Angels
The Leap of Faith
*One Man's True Story of How he Took the
Leap into the World of Angels*

Angels
The Leap of Faith
*One Man's True Story of How he Took the
Leap into the World of Angels*

Robert Woolley

ATHENA PRESS
LONDON

ANGELS – THE LEAP OF FAITH
*One Man's True Story of How he Took the
Leap into the World of Angels*
Copyright © Robert Woolley 2010

All Rights Reserved

ISBN 978 1 84748 757 5

First published 2010 by
ATHENA PRESS
Queen's House, 2 Holly Road
Twickenham TW1 4EG
United Kingdom

Printed for Athena Press

Acknowledgements

As this is a book about those beautiful celestial beings that we call angels, my heartfelt thanks must first of all go to them for never deserting me, and for always being there. Amhiel, Bellina and Chrystal – this book is especially for you.

A big thank you also to the spirit guides that have worked with me throughout my life.

From an earthly perspective, I would like to thank my mum and dad for all of the many lessons that they have taught me.

My sincere thanks also go to the many spiritual teachers that I have come across on my travels.

My children – Kerry, Hayley and Steven – and my grandchildren – Thomas, Benjamin, William and Matthew – this book is also for you.

And to my darling wife, Jackie, thank you for all your steadfast support. Here's to the rest of our life in this world, and to the life after that, beyond the veil.

Contents

Childhood Experiences

I have sometimes heard people ask others, 'What is your earliest childhood memory?' Well, for me, that is when it all began. It was December 1957, and I was two and a half years old. My earliest memory was in an ambulance, being taken back home after spending a week in hospital after having my tonsils taken out.

I clearly remember sitting in the back of the ambulance with an ambulance man, and with another driving the vehicle. The man who was in the back of the ambulance with me was very nice and kept me occupied all the way home by asking me about my hospital stay.

I still had a sore throat and it made it rather difficult to talk freely. At that stage, my family lived in an area just outside of Portsmouth called Paulsgrove. It was a very poor area and most of the houses were council houses or council flats. It was, though, an area where children could play freely outside their house and in the street without any worries.

While approaching Paulsgrove, I heard the ambulance driver shout through to his colleague in the back of the vehicle that he was not sure of the directions to the house where I lived. At that precise moment, the most remarkable thing happened. The man in the back with me became surrounded in flashing lights. There were all colours of light evident. I vividly remember seeing red, green, blue, yellow, violet and all shades of differing colours. I sat looking at this man in total amazement; it was my first vivid recollection of seeing something spiritual. Although at that stage, of course, I had no idea what I was seeing. The lights around the man seemed to be pulsating and moving in all sorts of directions. I suppose I could best describe them as balls of light, about the size of tennis balls but with no clear outer edges, and all of the lights seemed to be blurring in and out of focus.

While I sat transfixed, looking at these lights, I was aware of the two ambulance men talking to each other but their conversation was almost distant in nature as I sat looking at these wonderful lights. Shortly thereafter, the lights began to separate and, towards the back of the ambulance, three clear individual lights began to appear. I had no idea what I was seeing but these three individual lights then took on human appearances. I can clearly recall the image to this day. The three individual lights had developed into human forms, which became totally separated and detached as three individual beings. The middle of these beings was golden in colour and the two outer beings seemed to be more of a silvery nature. I did not know at the time, but this was my first recalled experience of seeing angels.

I know this to be a fact because I still see these three beautiful angelic beings even to this day. At that time, of course, I did not know they were angels and I certainly did not know their names, but later on in this book, I will explain who these angels are in much more detail.

The angel that was standing in the middle said to me, 'Robert, your driver is a little lost. Perhaps it is time we helped him.'

I could tell the angels were saying this in a fairly humorous way and the nature was jolly and light. They told me to say out loud the direction that the angels told me. I said exactly what the angels told me to say but I have absolutely no idea whether the two ambulance men took any notice of what I was saying at all. After all, who could expect a child of two and a half to know his way back home?

Fairly soon after that, the ambulance arrived outside the house we lived in and I was taken indoors. I do not recall saying anything about the experience within the ambulance to anybody at that time. In fact, I have no recollection of the house I was taken back to, and which was the family home, which is rather surprising seeing as I so clearly remember the incident within the ambulance.

About a year later, in 1958, the family moved to Falmouth Road, which again was a council house in Paulsgrove. I think at that time this particular house was called a prefab. Both of my parents were hard-working, working-class people. My mother did a wide variety of part-time jobs to try to supplement the family income while looking after the four children. I have a brother who is two years older than me, and two sisters who are two and four years younger. My parents' names are Stuart and Rosemary, my brother's name is Michael and my two sisters' names are Susan and Karen.

When we moved to Falmouth Road, my parents only had three children at that stage, with Michael having been born in 1953, me in 1955 and Susan in 1957. Karen wasn't born until 1960. Even though I was only about three and a half when we moved into this house, I remember the house relatively clearly. It was rather small, with a downstairs family room, a downstairs kitchen and the bedrooms upstairs.

We had no luxuries in the house, with both of my parents working hard to provide us with the basic living essentials. The house had an outside toilet and a rather large garden. I expect the garden was really not that large, but between the ages of three to seven, while living there, the garden seemed enormous to me. I certainly have no knowledge of my parents' finances at the time but obviously it was a very tough period for them and they struggled to have any cash whatsoever even to buy basic foods.

I remember eating bread and jam quite often as a meal, and it must have been very tough for my parents to survive with the children on such a shortage of money. While remembering bread and jam as forming a significant part of our diet at that time, I also recall having my childhood baths in a tin bath, which was put on the draining board on the sink in the kitchen. My mother used to boil a kettle of water and put that in the tin bath, then mix it with cold tap water to provide a lukewarm bath. I did, however, used to love our house in Falmouth Road and I had many angel and spirit experiences there.

At the age of about four, one sunny afternoon I was playing out in the garden. There were some bushes at the end of the garden and I could see lights flickering all around one particular bush. I went over to explore and again the lights started to move around, almost in a rhythmic dance, and began to form into the three angels that I had previously seen in the ambulance. The angel in the middle seemed to do most of the talking. I could see the three angels standing in the garden, and being so small myself, it is perhaps hard to accurately reflect their size but they seemed absolutely enormous to me. They were certainly much bigger than my father, who was about five foot eight inches tall, and I would estimate these angels to be in the region of about eight foot tall.

The angel in the middle presented himself as a male, and he had long flowing brown hair, a long white cloak and had on a necklace with its main feature being a beautiful blue stone.

The angel asked me to sit down and I remember sitting cross-legged in the middle of the garden looking at these fascinating beings. The angel said that he wanted to show me some of the wonderful things that lived in my garden at that time. They asked me to approach a grassed verge that we had, which butted on to a side of a fence. They asked me to move the grass down to one side so that I could see towards the roots of the grass, which were close to the fence perimeter. As I did this, I saw something that I had not seen previously but I would soon see many of, and that was a slow-worm. I did not know that they were called slow-worms at the time but in later years the angels would show me many slow-worms, lizards and other such creatures that were all around my garden.

The angels asked me to pick the slow-worm up and to look at it and to feel its texture. I must admit I was rather reluctant to do this because as I went to touch it, it wriggled and started to curl up into a ball. The angels laughed as I leapt back in a bit of shock. They asked me not to be afraid and just to pick the slow-worm up gently and tenderly and to feel its texture and to look at it closely. Again, I remember putting my hand down towards the slow-worm and I could see my fingers trembling as I got closer to it. The angels were all at this stage talking to me and giving me moral support.

While writing this book, I can even laugh at this myself but at the time this was no laughing matter. I once again touched the slow-worm and gently began to pick it up. Just as I did this, it once again formed itself tightly into a ball around my hand and fingers and it felt like it was getting firmer, as it was squeezing my fingers together. I let out a shriek as I dropped it on the floor. Again, the angels found this rather humorous and I remember them laughing as one of them said to me, 'Robert, please do not be afraid of something that is so beautiful. This is a gift from God; it cannot and will not harm you in any way.'

Even with the moral support that the angels were giving me, I still found it rather difficult to pick up the slow-worm, but I did try one more time. This time I did not even reach as far as I did on the previous occasion, as just as I was about to pick it up, once again, it rolled into a circle.

There was no doubt that I was feeling real fear at this stage and I said to the angels that I could not pick it up, and could they not show me what they wanted to show me without me touching it. Up to this point, I had always seen these three angels together and mainly spoken to the male angel in the middle. The other two angels were both female in appearance. The one standing on the left had shoulder-length black hair, and the one on the right had long blonde hair. The angel that was standing to the left of the one in the middle took a step forward to me and gently touched me on the side of the face. I felt such love and warmth flooding through my veins as the angel said to me, 'The love that we give you is the same love that that slow-worm you are reluctant to pick up gives to you. Just open your heart to feel it.'

I have always remembered those words, although it was going to take a long time before I could appreciate the beauty of the meaning behind them. The angels said, 'Robert, we will go now and leave you to play in the garden,' and just as I looked up at them, they gently vanished. Even though at that stage in my life I still had no understanding of what I was seeing or hearing, I did feel the warmth and the love from the angels every time I met them.

What I did not understand at that time, however, is that only a few people would be seeing them in the same form that I was. Looking back, I was having truly unique experiences that I was taking for granted and treating as the norm, without ever realising that not everybody was seeing the same things that I was. In later life, I certainly realised how fortunate I was, and indeed am, in seeing and hearing angels with such clarity.

Following that afternoon when I saw the angels in the garden, they visited me on many occasions in a similar vein, either outside in the garden or inside our house. I suppose now, looking back, it may well be that the main reason I loved our house so much was because it coincided with the beginning of where I was seeing and talking to the angels on a regular basis. It would be impossible to see the angels as frequently as I was seeing them and not be touched by their love and their warmth. I am sure that the energy that they presented also made the energy of the house so loving.

While seeing the angels pretty often from that moment on, it went up to a new level once I started school. In September 1960, at the age of five, I had my first day of school at Paulsgrove West Infants' School. I was a very skinny boy with blond hair and I was also very shy. I could talk to angels freely and listen to them intently but I did not have the same level of confidence when it came to talking to people. I vividly remember my first day of school, which was more of an autumn day than a summer's day. I was taken to school wearing, among other things, a duffel coat and short trousers. I was shown into the classroom and I stood by the door looking at all the other children playing but all I wanted to do was to go back home.

The teacher came to greet me. She was a lovely lady and I'm sorry that I do not remember her name, but she tried to welcome me and make me feel at ease. She asked me to sit in one of the children's chairs and to watch the others play. I did this for a few minutes. The teacher then approached me and asked me whether I would like to take my coat off and join in with the other children. I flatly refused to do this and remember putting my hands in my duffel coat pockets, pulling the hood over my head and trying to immerse myself in the coat, as if trying to vanish from the classroom. The teacher was still very nice to me and let me keep my coat on and continue to watch the other children. A few minutes later, she approached once again and asked if I wanted to play in the little sandpits they had out in the middle of the room. Again, I looked down at the floor and said, 'No, thank you.'

I just wanted to go home. Some time went by and the teacher started the normal school activities. She asked the other children to sit on the chairs or to sit on the floor cross-legged while she did the attendance register. It was at this stage that I began to notice the most incredible sight. Around every single child I could see flashing lights. Some were gold, some were silver, some were white and some were other colours, but generally they were gold, silver or white. They were like flickering lights, very small in size; the sparks you get off a sparkler would probably be an accurate comparison. These lights were generally around the children's heads and shoulders.

I sat open-mouthed, looking at this. I had no idea what I was seeing, but I soon realised that I was not looking at the children but was more interested in looking at these lights. It made me smile to see the way the lights flickered and moved around the children's heads. Some children just had one light flashing around them, others had two or three, but on average it was about two lights around each child. I remember also looking at the teacher, wondering why there were no lights around her. This was later to be explained to me.

While watching the lights around the children, I suddenly heard a voice coming from my right. I turned round to look but there was nobody there. The voice said, 'Robert, you are among friends. Please take your coat off and join in with the other children.' I was reluctant to do this but I felt compelled to actually start to take my coat off and follow the advice of the words I had just heard.

The teacher saw me start to take my coat off and approached me. She took the coat to hang it on the coat peg. As she was walking away, the voice coming from my right said, 'You are truly among friends. This is the time when you will start to learn the things you will need to know as a human being. We will supplement all of this, with all of the things you need to know as a spirit.'

The rest of the day passed without incident and I tried to join in with school life and was encouraged to play along with the other children. I also had the benefit of watching these lights around the children's heads. I said nothing of this to anybody. In fact, the time has now come for a major confession: I have never told anybody of my childhood spiritual experiences. In fact, I have never told anybody of most of my spiritual and angelic experiences, even as an adult.

I cannot fully explain why I have never told anybody (even my family) of the vast majority of things I have seen and heard in my life. I have seen and communicated with countless angels. I see these angels as clearly as I see human beings. I hear what these angels say to me as clearly as I would hear another human being talking to me.

I think there are two reasons for this. The first is that the times I said what I had seen with angels during my school years used to get me into trouble and that may have created a learnt behaviour in me to keep these things to myself, which I have continued to do in adult life.

The second reason is that, fairly early on in my school life, the angels did tell me not to say anything to anybody about some of the things they were talking to me about and some of the experiences that I had had with them. It was not clear at that time why they asked me to hold back on saying anything, and even to this day I can't fully explain why they asked me to keep things quiet. But I felt safe in their presence and I was happy to go along with the vow of silence.

The angels have now said that I have reached the point where that vow of silence has to be broken. I now want to document, through this book, some of the many experiences I have had with angels, and also spirits, so that this can act as a permanent record of these experiences, but more importantly I truly trust that some of the writings within this book will act as a stepping stone for others to take the leap into the world of angels. To do so can provide joy, love and abundance for every fibre of your being. Both you and the angels around you can benefit enormously from this leap… or even from a small step.

When I was aged about six, and by this time it would have been 1961, my mother allowed me to play outside the front of our house. While most of the area was of pavement and concrete, there was an area of about fifty yards by twenty yards that was all grass and in the shape of a triangle. My brother Michael and I, and the other young children of the area, used this as a place of play where we could do all the normal things that boys and girls would do at that age. We would make daisy chains, play football and would also treat the outer perimeter of the grass as a race-track, where we could race each other around the outside.

One evening in 1961 – and it must have been summertime because we were outside playing and it was relatively warm – my brother suggested that we have some races running around the grass perimeter. Michael said he would act as the starter and stand by what we then said would be the winning line, and I and two other boys would run around the outside of the grass to see who could win the race. I think at that time we suggested that there would be three laps in this race.

The two other boys and I keenly lined up on the start line and Michael said, 'Three, two, one, go,' and the race began. While I was a very skinny boy and slight in nature, I was quite a good runner for my age and I set off eagerly to do my best in the race. When we got to the end of the first lap, which was probably only a matter of minutes at most, I was in second position. All three of us were still relatively close in proximity and were quite evenly matched. We then proceeded to complete lap two and I moved myself into first place. Halfway round the final third lap, I looked over my shoulder and the other two boys were jogging rather than running and I built up a clear lead. I remember feeling all excited about the prospect of winning the race. As we were coming around the final bend, my brother was saying, 'It's OK, you've won. You can slow down now,' and that's exactly what I did. I just jogged towards the winning line, feeling very pleased with myself.

Suddenly, out of nowhere, one of the other two boys sprinted past me and overtook me just before the winning line, which put me into second place. It may seem strange for a six-year-old to feel this, but I was truly distraught. I was in floods of tears as I ran towards my house. My mother opened the front door and I ran in crying. I was totally inconsolable.

She said it was good that I came in, as it was now time for tea and a bath. I saw her pick up the metal tin bath we had, which can only have been three foot long and a couple of feet high, and she started to boil the kettle for the water. I got in the bath on top of the draining board and was still crying inconsolably and my mother asked me what was the matter. I told her that Michael had told me that I was winning the race, and I slowed down and as a result of that, I allowed myself to be overtaken. I was so desperate to win and so sad that I didn't. My mother tried to console me by saying it didn't matter, and I could perhaps win next time but for me it was my first feeling of losing.

Looking back now, it is incredible that I had such strong feelings over something of such a minor nature but for me at the time it meant everything. Ten minutes later, Michael came in for his bath and tea (again, I think we had jam sandwiches that night). Michael was laughing and treating the whole incident as a joke. To this day I still don't think he realises just how distraught I was. Incredibly that one incident served as a catalyst for some major angel intervention later that night.

I remember lying in my bed, still thinking of the race and the sheer sadness of it all, when suddenly standing in front of me was an incredible sight. I saw this deep purple colour and it seemed to fill the entire bedroom, and out of this deep purple came the most majestic angel that I had ever seen. He seemed to be enormous.

The house we lived in didn't have very high ceilings, but even so this angel filled the entire height of the room and was clearly over eight feet in height. I could not see his feet and remember wondering how was he standing there when I could see from about knee height upwards and yet below that was just a blur of purple light. This angel held out his hand and said, 'Robert, today you have learnt an important lesson. It is a lesson that will stand you in good stead for the future, and I have come to you today to reinforce this message and to teach you other things that you will need to know.'

Up to this point, most of my conversations with the angels had been with them talking to me as a normal person would, and me hearing them clearly and me responding either by thought or by me speaking as well. On this occasion, I could hear all of his words and yet I could not see his mouth moving. He was also answering my questions before I'd even posed them.

This clearly taught me that angels could communicate through thought equally well as through speech. The angel told me that he was called Archangel Michael. He said he was an archangel, which at that time meant nothing to me other than he looked bigger and certainly felt more powerful than the angels I had seen to date.

He said, 'Robert, I have come to you to surround you in a shield of protection, which will help you now and in later life too.'

I remember thinking at the time that I did not know what I was being protected from and Archangel Michael immediately picked up these thoughts and said, 'You will be protected from all things seen and unseen.' Again, at this stage, that meant nothing to me.

Archangel Michael talked to me through thought about something which I later learnt to be spiritual law, the law of cause and effect, the law of like attracting like, the law of equal and opposite, and all other such things. He told me that the sadness I had felt at losing the race earlier against the other boys had been offset by the sheer joy of the boy that had won the race. Archangel Michael told me the boy that won the race had never won anything in his life, and would go through his life never winning anything again. It was the one time when he was going to win something and the joy that he felt at winning that race would live with him for ever.

I remember feeling staggered at this and I regret to say that I sent a thought to Archangel Michael that I still wished it was me that had won the race. Archangel Michael smiled at that and said that I would learn.

Archangel Michael said that he would be visiting me many times in the next few years to teach me a lot of things regarding protection and other things I would need to know later on in life. I watched in amazement as the room changed back from being a deep purple to a dull dusky colour. When he left, my breathing changed quite considerably and I think this was as a consequence of the sheer power that Archangel Michael possessed.

Something just as incredible happened later that night. I do not know whether or not this was coincidental, or whether this was linked to Archangel Michael's visit, but I drifted off to sleep unaware of what was shortly to follow. I woke halfway through the night, having no idea what the time was but I was being shaken on my shoulder. I looked up and through bleary eyes I could see a lady standing before me, which initially I thought was my mother, but I soon realised that this was one of the three angels that used to visit me regularly.

She beckoned me by waving her finger and asked me to sit up. This I did. Once I was upright the most amazing experience of my early childhood happened. I was suddenly no longer sitting up on my bed in my bedroom; instead, I was sitting around a fire. At the time I had no idea where I was or how I had even got there. I looked all around me and there were others sitting around this fire also, but they were all dressed differently to me.

There was a man speaking, and he had a great big headdress on, which was full of feathers. I was looking at the others around the fire and I realised that these people all looked similar. The man who was speaking spoke with great authority and wisdom. He was much older than the others. Some of them had pieces of cloth around their head; some of them had the odd feather. But the elderly man that was doing all of the talking was draped in feathers everywhere.

I did not know where I was at all, but I sat there intently listening to this man speak. I cannot explain this, but he was speaking in a language I did not know, but I understood every word he said. It was in later years that the angels explained to me that I had been taken to a Native American campfire, where a great chief was talking to some of his braves about the battles that lay ahead for them and their race. How they had to face these battles with strength, courage and belief but also, even in times of hardship, that they needed to forever praise the great spirits and to work as one with nature.

I did not realise at that stage the importance of what I was being shown, and to what I was being party to, but I consider it one of the greatest honours that I have ever had bestowed upon me to have had the privilege of sitting around this Native American campfire and to listen to this great man speak.

I suddenly then became aware that I was back sitting on my bed and in front of me was the angel that had taken me to this campfire. She said I would be going back there many times and she smiled as she said, 'You can call it your second home.' This is a privilege that I hold to this day.

I have listed in this chapter some of the childhood experiences I have had in relation to angels. In some of the later chapters I will also list some of the many things the angels have said to me, in relation to the ability that is within all of us, should we wish to develop it, to contact angels at will.

While some of the experiences I have written were not understandable to me (as a result of my very young age when they occurred), once I left infant school and attended junior and senior school, then a lot more of the mystery that surrounded angels in my early years was about to unravel.

In 1962, my mother and father decided to move from our house in Falmouth Road to a place called St Paul's Square in Southsea, which is in Portsmouth. About a week before we moved, at the age of seven, I was sitting alone at the bottom of the stairs when out of nowhere a beautiful angel appeared in front of me. I instantly recognised her as the angel that had led me to the Native Americans' camp. She was one of the three angels that I had seen often in my childhood years. She asked me not to be sad that we were leaving our home as many more exciting adventures were about to be presented to me. She told me that her name was Chrystal and that she was my guardian angel. This was a term I had never heard of before but it sounded nice to me, and I was happy to accept that this beautiful angel Chrystal was my guardian angel.

A strange thing happened at that moment because whereas previously angels had presented themselves in front of me and communicated with me from either the front or to the side of me, Chrystal actually sat on the stairs next to me. I found this very comforting. She said that I would be leaving the house that I currently lived in and moving to a new place and that I would also be leaving my current school and going to a new one. She could sense that this filled me with fear and that I perceived this to be a rather large ordeal. She placed her two hands on my two hands and looked into my eyes and said, 'Do not be afraid, dear child. We will be with you wherever you are, for ever.' As I looked into her eyes I sensed this overwhelming love was running through me, coursing through every vein in my body.

Chrystal said that the school I was going to was a good school, and that the angels would be waiting for me there and would be showing me some wonderful sights. She also said we would not be living at our next home for very long and that we would be moving to a much bigger house within a few years. I remember asking Chrystal whether my brother Michael, sister Susan and new sister Karen would be coming with me when we moved. Chrystal laughed and she said, 'All of your family will be moving and many exciting things will be waiting for you.'

This was my first recollection of having a very deep conversation with the angels. I then started to ask who else was seeing the angels. In particular I remember asking, 'Does my brother Michael or my sister Susan see you?' knowing that at that stage, in 1962, Michael would have been nine and Susan five. During my discussion I assumed that Karen would not be seeing the angels, as she was only two: a silly assumption considering my own early experiences!

Chrystal laughed quite loudly at this and said that all children could see and hear angels but that many just did not realise it. She said that in this instance, while Michael, Susan and Karen would have had their own angel experiences in their very early years, they would not recollect their experiences for reasons that she was not willing to explain. Chrystal continued by saying to me that it was important that I didn't say anything to my brother or sisters, or indeed my parents, about any of my angel experiences. She said something at the time that I thought was rather strange. She said that the experiences were to be kept between the angels and myself, and that only when the time was right would I be encouraged to fully speak my truth.

Little did I realise that it would take another forty-six years before I had the opportunity to fully open my heart and speak my truth about the wonderful experiences that I have had with those beautiful beings that we call angels.

The School Years

In late 1962 the family moved to St Paul's Square, Southsea. I do not recall much about the move other than feeling sadness at leaving our previous home in Paulsgrove, where I had many happy memories both from being a child and also the angelic visits. By this time, Michael was nine, I was seven, Susan was five and Karen was two. We moved to a top-floor flat, which in comparison to our previous house seemed rather small to me. The family's finances had obviously not improved at all as both my parents were still working very hard trying to keep the family fed.

Once we had fully moved into the flat, it became apparent to me that I was going to miss the garden of our previous home. I had many happy memories of playing in the garden, meeting with the angels and learning some of the wonderful things about nature they taught me. I was particularly going to miss the talks that we had on nature, and specifically the sights they showed me with regards to the slow-worms and lizards, which were abundant at that time.

I was also going to miss playing on Portsdown Hill, which is a hill about three hundred feet high, very close to our house in Falmouth Road. In fact, this house was only about one hundred yards from the bottom of Portsdown Hill. I remember Michael and I playing for hours on the hill and in particular trying to catch lizards. I was very successful at doing that, which in no small part was due to the angels showing me where most of them were!

I would slowly approach some of the bushes on top of the hill looking for lizards, and on many occasions I knew exactly what bush to go to, because the bush was illuminated by the energy of an angel. I used to creep up to those bushes very slowly and carefully, knowing that a lizard would be out basking in the sunlight and that the angels were happy for me to see and catch lizards. The angels knew by that stage that I was quite happy to catch them, hold them in my hands, study them and let them go again.

I often used to think back to those early days when the angels first showed me the slow-worm that I was too terrified to pick up, and here I was now, just a couple of years later, quite happy to catch lizards by diving on them with my hands cupped, and then holding and looking at them before letting them go.

The lizards always became calm and relaxed while they were in my hands, which at the time I used to feel was strange, as I would have thought that as soon as you loosened your grip on them, they would jump off into the grass and scurry away. On nearly every occasion, I could open my hands and the lizard would be quite happy to lie there while I gently stroked its head and neck before placing it on the ground to let it go where I had previously caught it. It was only in later life that I realised that by holding the lizards like I had, I was in fact giving them angel healing. This is why they were quite happy to lie there and receive the healing, as opposed to running away immediately. I knew I particularly missed this element of my childhood now that we were living in the top-floor flat.

We did have an external balcony that we could stand on, but of course this was no substitute for a natural garden. I do not recall seeing any angels for at least a week once we had moved into our new home, but this did not concern me, as I knew that I would be seeing them again shortly.

I presume I could not have been the brightest seven-year-old on the planet, and I clearly remember my induction at the new infants' school that I started in 1962. It was at a school called Cottage Grove Infants in Southsea. My brother and I were taken to the headmaster for a school induction for him to test our ability before deciding what class to put us in. He asked us a few basic questions and in particular I remember one arithmetic question, which was what is three multiplied by three? When he asked this, standing behind him was an angel. The angel was talking to me at the same time as the headmaster. The angel said, 'This is indeed a very powerful angel number.'

Whether or not I was distracted by the angel, or whether it was my own inability to be able to work something out quickly in my head, I don't know but I confidently said 'six'. I was, of course, asked to have another go and once again I worked out in my head that three multiplied by three was six. I'm not sure who was most surprised with my answer, the headmaster or the angel standing behind him!

Fortunately my brother who was sitting next to me on my right-hand side said that the answer was nine. I looked at him incredulously wondering how he got that, as I was very confident in my own answer of six. The headmaster said he had seen enough and fortunately both of us passed whatever was necessary to be admitted to the school, infants for me and junior school for Michael.

When we were walking out of the headmaster's office, the angel that had been standing behind the headmaster was standing in front of me in the corridor. He said not to worry that I had got the number wrong – in fact I think the angel found that quite amusing – but he said the true answer was indeed the answer that Michael had given. He continued by saying that the number nine was an important number to the angels and they would explain to me why that was so important at a later date.

I was only in Cottage Grove infant school for a matter of months before starting the junior school along with my elder brother. One of the things I most noticed about the difference between my old and new school was the light around all of the children. It was in later years that I realised that what I had been seeing was the guardian angels of these children. Also angels came into the classroom to play and support the children on a frequent basis. I strongly believe the sweetness, the innocence, the naivety of youth played a major part in creating the right energy to enable the angels to naturally gravitate to the school classrooms. I suppose this is best illustrated by a saying that an angel gave to me in later years, which I think sums up perfectly why angels naturally gravitate to children.

An angel said to me, which must have been when I was in my thirties, 'If you want to live with angels, you need to make your world, your thoughts and your feelings more like theirs. If you truly live in the heart, and have the highest good of all concerned in all of your actions, then the angels will naturally gravitate to you.'

I see that as a clear indication that children, who naturally live in the moment, and play freely with a smile on their face and laughter in their hearts, are a natural energy magnet for angels. Perhaps we that are now in adulthood could still learn an awful lot from children, if only we spent some time to look at them closely and learn the many lessons they so naturally and so readily demonstrate to us.

In my first year of junior school, I used to sit next to a girl with long blonde hair. Sadly, I do not recall her name now but she had the most beautiful of guardian angels. I knew with great certainty that it was a guardian angel that I saw, as her guardian angel used to talk freely with my guardian angel Chrystal on many occasions.

I found the teachers to be extremely friendly and helpful and thoroughly enjoyed my time at both the infant and junior schools, experiencing numerous angel visits during my time there. I had put on no real weight in the intervening years at junior school, and people were still concerned over it. I do not know if the concern over my lack of weight was raised by my parents or the school teachers but I remember at some stage during my junior school attendance that I had to go to the chemist every Saturday morning to get weighed so that my weight could be monitored.

When I went to the chemist for my very first visit, my mother came with me, and I remember the chemist saying to my mother when he first saw me, 'My word, this is a skinny one. I think this boy will end up being six foot six inches tall and six inches wide.' Looking back now, the chemist was not too far wrong with me being six foot four inches tall, though I can happily say I am more than six inches wide!

After the first few visits to the chemist, I used to walk there alone from our flat, which was about a mile away. I had to take my record card with me to get weighed. In fact, I felt quite special in doing this, and always had great glee in opening the chemist door, walking into the shop and being greeted by the staff ready for my weekly weigh-in. I have no idea what my weight was at the time, but obviously I must have been severely underweight.

Most weeks during the weigh-in a variety of angels used to appear and they were always in a happy, jolly mood, as indeed angels always are. They used to fill the chemist shop with humour and love. I also used to see angels regularly at my junior school and I used to enjoy playtimes and lunchtimes as I could go out into the playground and walk around and talk with the angels. I found it more and more difficult to communicate with the angels while in class, as it was difficult for me to concentrate on what the teachers were saying and what the angels were saying and doing. Even with this distraction, I was quite good in junior school and achieved a relatively high standard in all of my work, especially in relation to reading, writing and arithmetic. I give the teachers great credit for that and obviously came a long way from the days when I first started when I was convinced that three times three equalled six!

One sunny day out in the playground when I was about nine, an angel appeared in front of me and said, 'Robert, you are becoming a bit of a loner. We would like you to mix more and play more with your friends.'

I was a bit taken aback with this. I said to the angel that I loved coming out to play and I loved to listen and watch the angels, and while I was happy to play with the other children, I took more delight out of talking to the angels. The angel that presented itself to me said it was very important that I mixed and played with the other children, as this was an essential part of my development. She said that the angels themselves would always be with me, and around me, and it would be in later years when they would teach me more of the things I needed to know.

I must admit I was a bit upset with this, as I felt I naturally gravitated more to the angels than I did to the other children. This point was obviously picked up by a couple of the teachers, because at one stage, on one particular afternoon, I was called into the school office and told that it had become apparent that I used to walk 'aimlessly' around the playground without mixing with the other children. It may have been rather foolish at that time but I blurted out to the teacher that I wasn't walking around 'aimlessly' on my own, but that I was talking to the angels.

I could see she was shocked by this and she asked me what I meant by saying that. I said to her that I saw lots of angels in the school, and out in the playground, and it was with the angels that

I used to talk during free time. I was absolutely amazed when the teacher told me to stop making up stories and to listen to what she was saying. She repeated her desire for me to play more with the other children and when she finished talking, she said I could go now and finished by saying, 'Remember, you must not make up these stories.'

I was both shocked and saddened by this. This was my first experience of telling somebody the truth of what I was seeing and hearing and having scorn poured upon that. Throughout the following weeks, every time I went out to play, especially at lunchtime, I could see the teachers looking at me. I was well aware they wanted me to mix with the other children, and of course the angels wanted that, too. At this stage I had perhaps reverted to being rather shy, so rather than approach groups of other children and try to mingle, I began to realise that I could look at the other children and, just by thought, attract one or two of them over to me. We would stand around in either pairs or a group of three, just talking about normal childhood things.

To this day, I have no idea how I managed to attract the other children to me, just by thought, and no doubt the angels played a major part in achieving this. I was still having weight issues and was still very skinny compared to some of the other children. My parents were working every hour they could in order to feed us, but obviously the welfare state at that stage was nowhere near as supportive as it is now.

I remember being out some late afternoons and early evenings, walking around some of the local fish and chip shops in Southsea and going inside, obviously penniless, but asking whoever was behind the counter whether they had any scraps they could give me. Some of the time, one of my friends used to be with me when we did this and it was a great delight when we were given a small bag of batter scraps. We were incredibly excited on the odd occasion when there was either a piece of sausage or even the odd few chips in with the scraps they gave us. This was a big highlight for us.

I do not think my thin body was in any way caused purely by malnutrition or insufficient food; I think it was more a reflection of both my brother and I being incredibly energetic. We were always out playing, constantly running and growing fairly tall in height and our voracious appetite was more of a reflection of our energetic lifestyle, as opposed to insufficient food quality or quantity at home.

My mother had quite a few part-time jobs to supplement the family income, whereas my father, throughout his working career, was quite a sickly person and had a lot of stomach problems, especially in relation to stomach ulcers and was often more at home sick than he was at work.

On one particular day in the flat where we lived, I remember sitting on my bed and being alone in the flat. I was reminiscing about Portsdown Hill and our old house and garden. I was suddenly joined once again by the trio of angels entering the room together. One of these was my guardian angel, Chrystal, and I asked her who the other two angels were. This is where I had my first formal teaching. Chrystal told me that while the angels appeared as two females and one male, angels themselves are neither sex; they are something that we now call androgynous, which means they can be either sex or neither sex. They have the ability to present themselves in the energy that is required at the time. For example, if you are in a situation where you need protection, it is most likely that an angel will present itself in masculine form. Whereas, if you needed sensitivity and tender-ness, the angel was more likely to present itself in a feminine form.

My guardian angel Chrystal always presents herself in the feminine form, and in the majority of cases with the other two angels that I often see with her, one is female and one is male. Chrystal told me also that angels do not have names the same way that we do, or at least not in any way that we could understand, and that they operate on something called a vibration. She did say that, as we like to know names and be introduced as such, she would gladly tell me the names of the other two. So for the first time, at the age of ten, I found out the names of the three angels that I had first seen in the ambulance taking me back home from my tonsil operation.

Chrystal said that the male angel was called Amhiel and the other female angel was called Bellina. I know names are not important to angels but it was really quite a considerable impact on me to be told the names of these three celestial beings. Chrystal, my main guardian angel, and Amhiel and Bellina, the two angels who were often with her. Interestingly, when I do see them all together, Amhiel is always in the middle, with Chrystal to his left and Bellina to his right.

In early 1965, during a cold winter's night, I was once again awoken by the majestic presence of Archangel Michael. The room was illuminated once again with the most beautiful purple colour as Archangel Michael stood at the end of my bed. He was as awesome as I remembered him that first time I saw him. His power, strength and courage was, and is, immeasurable. This time he was accompanied by another angel, who said to me that within about a year the family would be moving from the flat we currently lived in to a much bigger house, and in this house I would see the angels on a daily basis for some very important things that needed to be shown to me and for some very important things I needed to do.

By this stage I had learnt to communicate clearly with the angels by thought, as well as speaking normally to them as though they were humans. Generally, whenever I was alone with angels, I would always talk to them as I would talk to anybody else; it was only if I was in the company of others that I communicated to them through thought. They were quite happy to talk to me audibly or again through telepathy. I asked the angel with Archangel Michael why we needed to move again and what it was they wanted me to do. The angel said something I hadn't heard of at the time, but have heard many times since, which is, 'Everything is in divine perfect order and everything is as it should be.' With that, Archangel Michael and the angel that was supporting him gently vanished from the room.

Sure enough, during 1965 the family moved to a house in Orchard Road in Southsea. This seemed an enormous house in comparison to the flat we had just left. It was probably bigger than the original house we lived in at Falmouth Road. I remember the excitement I felt when I first entered the new house. Again, this was a council house but it was much more imposing than the flat we had just left. It had a small concreted-over front garden about six feet wide. When you opened the front door, you could see the hallway and stairs going up the right-hand side. Downstairs there was a lounge, a spare room, a dining room and kitchen. Outside of the kitchen was the external garden, which was just a bit smaller than I remember our previous house having.

The upstairs consisted of four bedrooms and a bathroom. We had come a long way since our outside toilet and small tin bath to a house with a separate bathroom and toilet all indoors, a luxury indeed. Little did I realise that the room that I have not yet mentioned was soon to have the most profound effect on my life. For downstairs in the hall there was a small, white, wooden partitioned door that led to a downstairs cellar. When you opened this partitioned door, there was a light switch, which illuminated the downstairs cellar. There must have been at least fifteen stairs down into the cellar and it was cold, dark and full of cobwebs, and almost the size of the downstairs floor plan. A large space indeed.

I remember when I first went down there, my childhood excitement at seeing a downstairs cellar was mixed with a feeling of doom and gloom as to the darkness contained within this cellar. It was here in the darkness of the cellar that many of my most profound childhood spiritual and angelic experiences would take place.

I did have some quite fond memories of certain aspects of living in Orchard Road. A couple of these surrounded the delivery of coal and also the rag and bone man. Once a week, normally on a Saturday morning, a coal lorry used to drive along the road and stop at most of the houses for delivery of coal. This was delivered in bags, although I do remember some of it being delivered loose and being tipped straight down coal cellars. Looking back, that is something you just don't see now, whereas in the sixties most people used to heat their houses with coal or log fires. Nowadays we are in the era of central heating! And even fonder memories of that time surrounded the rag and bone man, who used to come along the road, again on a once-a-week basis. I first heard the rag and bone man coming along by the sound of horses' hooves clattering along the road. The rag and bone man would be driving the cart, shouting out something in a fairly high-pitched voice. I later learned that he was shouting 'rag and bone' but the way he expressed that was 'rag and booone'.

I used to look out of the window to see him and his horse and sometimes would even go out and stand in the porchway to see him. I was always intrigued by the lights that were all around the horse. There seemed to be flickering lights around the horse's head, down his mane and along his back. These lights used to interweave with each other, which seemed to be just like a shoal of fish swimming all around him. It was truly incredible to witness this. Whenever the man stopped to carry out a collection of people's old clothing, or whatever was handed over to him, I was much more fascinated by the horse and the lights around it. The lights I saw were a wide variety of colours and used to weave in and out all around the horse, and there must have been hundreds of these flickers of light. I once asked Chrystal what these flickers of light were. She smiled at me and said there were many things of a spiritual nature that I could not yet understand, but I should take the time to look at the lights and enjoy what she described as 'the light show'. I duly did this every time I saw the rag and bone man with his horse. I did not ask the angels again what this was surrounding the horse, but the memory has remained with me to this day.

I still attended Cottage Grove Junior School and did so until the early summer of 1966. My academic ability had come on quite considerably and I took the eleven plus exam and passed it with flying colours. This enabled me to attend Northern Grammar School for Boys from September 1966 until July 1970.

There were many nights when I was asleep that I was awoken during the night to be once again taken on a visit to the Native American encampment. This happened on more occasions than I could count. It would have been well in excess of one hundred times. It was always the same format; I would be woken by the angel Chrystal, beckoned to lean forward and then I would find myself in the Native American encampment, once again sitting around the fire, listening to the elders speak their words of wisdom in a language I did not know but fully understood. On many occasions, while sitting around the campfire, I also explored some of the encampment. The tepees were magnificent. They seemed very large to me, much larger than I would have thought.

When you opened the front of the tepee it felt as though it was made of cowhide. You would go into the tepee and there would be a small fire, which caused some form of smoke within the tepee. I do not know if this was a cleansing activity but I witnessed this on many occasions.

I also saw Native Americans chanting and putting on ornamental designs around their body and paint on their faces. The encampment itself was near the base of some hills and mountains and there were trees pretty well all around. To the right-hand side of the tepees there was a lake with small canoe boats close to the encampment. At the back of the tepees to the left-hand side, in the trees close to the foot of the mountains, there was a fenced area where many horses were kept. The joy and excitement within this encampment was always so touching. There would often be children running around playing with a freedom I had never experienced before.

There would be young men sitting around the campfire, listening to the elders speak, and the females would be mixing herbs, carrying water and generally going about their day-to-day business. The thrill and excitement that was always evident within the encampment will remain with me until my dying day. On some occasions, the thrill and excitement would be replaced with tension and urgency. This was more evident in the latter years of my childhood. Looking back now, it is clear that this was at the time when the tribe in question was on some form of war footing. The energies of the encampment would change at these times.

The family were now settled in to our new house and I was beginning to get a little more confident about going down into the cellar. In the early days, my father put up a dartboard, which enabled Michael and me to go down to the cellar to play darts. We were not very good at this game but it did while away many an hour. Sometimes I would be led to the cellar by the angels to go down there alone and to turn the light off and sit in the darkness of the cellar and listen to some of their teachings. Initially I could not understand why they would want me to do this but that became clear later on.

The atmosphere in the cellar was often cold, dark and dank

and reflected some of my early childhood years when the family had it so tough. My mother was stalwart through all of her working life and did everything possible to give her four children love and affection and worked many hours to try to feed us. My father, who had also worked very long hours, suffered quite a bit of ill health, both physically and mentally. My father (who has now passed) often found it difficult to cope with the stress that having four young children would bring on him. While he tried to contain this stress, on many occasions it would erupt into sheer fury on his part. During my childhood years, my father, on many occasions, would vent his fury on me in a physical way. My mother often would try to prevent this, but she too would be subject to physical abuse.

My father was not a bad man at all; he worked hard for his family and tried to provide a roof over our head and food on our table at all times. There were many times when we went hungry as a family and had nothing to eat. I think that also contributed to the stress that he experienced. This, coupled with his degenerating physical and mental health, left him feeling inadequate and unable to cope. Maybe it was this that caused him to explode in anger and rage, which often resulted in physical abuse for me or my mother or both.

It would not be right to go into further details within this book. It was on one such occasion, however, when I was sitting in the cellar alone, having been led down there by an angel (not Chrystal but another female-formed angel), that I saw for the very first time a truly magnificent angel bedecked all in gold with a shimmering copper-coloured light all around. It was clear to me that this angel was a very powerful presence indeed. There were many angels in the cellar with me at that time but this one angel commanded all of my attention. It was a male energy. He was clearly ten foot tall and the aura around him was the brightest copper and gold light you could ever see. He had a gold necklace and most beautiful long flowing robes and long golden hair. He said his name was Archangel Gabriel. I knew I was in the presence of something awesome. Archangel Gabriel told me that the reason the angels wanted to meet me in the cellar was for me to be shown some very important teachings and to undertake some in-depth learning that I would need in later life.

Archangel Gabriel said to me that, while we were sitting in the darkness and could only see each other and the other angels present, the lesson I needed to learn was, 'out of the darkness will always come the light'. He asked me to always remember that no matter how dark my life was, no matter how low or desperate I felt, no matter how much pain I suffered, that out of that darkness will always come the light.

He said that light will always manifest itself as a bridge to the angels, and was there for me to call on any time. It was then that I could fully understand every issue surrounding my father. For out of the darkness he felt, and out of the darkness he brought on my mother and me at certain stages of his life, comes the light he is now in, and the light he is now bestowing on us, his family. Archangel Gabriel said he would be giving me guidance over the next few years, which would serve as a baseline for things I would need in future life. He also told me to enjoy the Native American visitations I had, knowing that these, coupled with all of the angels' work, would act as a mosaic of light that one day would be used to illuminate many others.

I told Archangel Gabriel that I used to feel a lot of fear in the cellar and still had that emotion with me on many occasions. Even though I had seen many angels down there, I still often felt fear being alone in the cellar. He said that those with the strongest light often have to carry the greatest darkness but whatever the darkness conjured up, it would always be overcome by the light. I was grateful for these words but in the years ahead, while living at Orchard Road, I still continued to feel a certain element of fear in that cold, dark cellar.

I asked Archangel Gabriel why the angels had first come to me in the ambulance on the way back home when I was two and a half years old.

He said, 'Robert, it is not the first occasion you have had of seeing us; it is just your first recollection of it.'

I was actually born at 10.10 p.m. on Sunday, 3 July 1955 at number four, Margate Road, Southsea, weighing eight pounds. Archangel Gabriel told me that I had been surrounded by angels from that moment forward and from preconception. At the time, I did not understand that comment.

Number four Margate Road has now unfortunately been demolished, so while I cannot ever visit the house of my birth, I can still visit the area where the house once stood. It was demolished in the mid-1950s and fairly close to that house lived my Auntie Jean and Uncle Reg (my Auntie Jean being my father's sister). On certain weekends, my brother and I went to stay with my Auntie Jean, which, looking back, I think was when my parents were having the most problems, either financially or emotionally.

On every occasion when I went to stay with Auntie Jean, she was always surrounded by angels. She had angelic presences all around her. Auntie Jean lived in a flat above the hairdressers she owned called Deb's Hair Fashion in Somerstown from the mid-1960s onwards. Auntie Jean was an excellent hairdresser and my brother and I had many happy memories of staying with her in the flat above her shop.

I thanked Archangel Gabriel by saying that the angels had always been with me but reiterated that I had only recollections of them from the time I was in the ambulance. Archangel Gabriel found this quite amusing as he said that I had had many angelic experiences in December 1957 while in Gosport's War Memorial Hospital when my tonsils were being taken out. Unfortunately, however, I have no recollection of this.

Just before Archangel Gabriel departed on this particular day, he said to me that when I started senior school in September 1966, many things would happen to me that would provide a firm foundation for future years, and that contact with the angels would increase considerably and they would communicate with me much more on an ongoing basis. Up until that time, a lot of the communications I had had with the angels were of a general nature and he said that some of the communications that would follow would be much more specific and targeted for things they wanted me to know. I readily accepted this and thanked him for his beautiful words. Little did I know how meaningful those words were from Archangel Gabriel. What started to happen from September 1966 onwards would transform my life for ever.

It was with great sadness that I left Cottage Grove Junior School. I really enjoyed my time there and I really enjoyed the many angel experiences I had. I also thought the teachers were very friendly and helpful and I made some quite close friends by the time I left the school.

I started at Northern Grammar School for Boys, which is in an area of Portsmouth called North End, in September 1966, at the age of eleven. A couple of weeks before I started, my mother took me out to buy the school uniform. Like most children starting senior school for the first time, I was quite nervous. I was fairly tall for my age and I was pleased when my mother bought me long trousers to wear as opposed to short ones. The uniform consisted of grey trousers, a white shirt, a yellow and black striped tie and a dark blazer.

A day or so before starting school, I remember sitting in my bedroom and felt very apprehensive about going to what I perceived to be 'big school'. I was suddenly aware of an angel presence in front of me and I opened my eyes and looked up and saw Angel Bellina standing right before me. She held out her hands in a supportive gesture and I placed my hands on top of her hands and immediately felt comforted. She told me that she could feel the apprehension and nerves that I was experiencing as a result of starting senior school and she told me not to worry and that everything would be fine. Of course, even though the angels used to say this sort of thing to me on a frequent basis, it didn't take away the human emotion that a child feels in the face of relatively major upheaval.

Angel Bellina has a different energy to Chrystal and Amhiel, with her energy being of a much more supportive and sensitive nature, whereas Amhiel is bolder and more forthright in both his energy and the things he says. Chrystal, however, also has a sensitive, caring energy, but she is more of a prompting and nudging nature. I would summarise the three different energies of these angels by saying Amhiel is bold, protecting, strong and courageous, Bellina is gentle, sensitive, supportive and caring, and finally Chrystal is sensitive and caring also, but with an emphasis on prompting and nudging me. I now look upon Amhiel as my protector, Bellina as my comforter and Chrystal as my prompter.

Angel Bellina always presents herself slightly differently to the other two that I regularly see. Chrystal, for example, has long blond hair, Amhiel has brown hair, and Bellina has shoulder-length black hair. She also invariably carries something with her, which reflects whatever energy she is trying to bring through at that particular time. For example, I have seen her fairly frequently carrying spiritual flowers, either a red rose or a white rose. The colours of the flowers that she often carries are almost impossible to describe. The sheer vividness of the colours is something that I have never seen in normal earthly colours. I do not know how it is possible that Bellina can present things that are coloured, but in different shades and colours to what we see on earth, but it is a fact.

On this particular occasion, she was carrying something of a silver colour in her right hand. I asked Bellina what this was that she was presenting to me at that time. Bellina said it was a spiritual pen, a pen made of citrine, which was a gift from Archangel Gabriel. It was presented to me to help with the writing that I would one day perform, to help get across the angels' message. I asked Bellina what writing she referred to, and she indicated that I would be performing some writing while at school, some writing when I left school and some writing in adulthood that would help to get across some of the messages of the angels.

Bellina told me that Archangel Gabriel often works with children and his primary source of energy is linked to giving guidance. He was, in fact, a key communicator for the angelic realms. I was very pleased to receive this pen at this stage, but having had so many interactions with the angels throughout my life, I tended at that stage to just take it all as a matter of course. It is only now that I am in adulthood that I am amazed and full of wonder at the majestic things that the angels do for us on a daily basis. It is just that most people are blissfully unaware of what the angels carry out daily for us. Looking back, I consider myself to be incredibly fortunate to have had these angelic experiences throughout my life, even though at the time I took them for granted.

Angel Bellina let me hold the pen for a short while, and it felt different to a normal pen inasmuch as it seemed to have a life of its own. It was pulsating with energy and the light around it flickered; it was almost as if the pen had an aura of its own. I held it for a couple of minutes and then passed the pen back to Bellina, who smiled at me and said once again not to be nervous about starting a new school and that the angels would be with me there, and would be so always. This did give me comfort, but obviously I still had those earthly nerves on my first day at school.

When I went to senior school on that day in September 1966, I must have felt almost as I did on my first day at infants' school, but this time I had no duffel coat to hide behind!

My brother was also at this school and I travelled with him on the bus to go there. I remember getting off the bus at the bus stop, which was about half a mile away from the school. The school was in a road called Mayfield Road, and the bus stopped right at the end of that particular road. My brother and I walked down it towards the school. There were many other children going to school on that day, and in particular I was looking around for any others that looked about my age. These stood out rather starkly from the other school children in that their uniforms were immaculate. They had that 'shop-bought' look and looked suitably pressed and smart. Most of the boys that went to school carried their school books in football club sports bags and it was only the new boys like myself that tended to carry their stuff in brand new school satchels.

As we approached the school on that first day, I noticed this very large building to my left, which my brother told me was the girls' school adjacent to the boys' school. We continued walking down the road and we eventually reached the gates of the school. As we entered, I paused for a few seconds and looked at the imposing shape of the school building. It was two storeys high and had an ornamental entrance. It looked more to me like a military building, where you would expect officers to walk up the stairs and to go through the big, imposing doors.

We went into the school doors and entered the main school corridor and I was amazed with the noise that was being emitted from the other children. There were children there from the age of eleven to sixteen and everybody we passed seemed to be talking at once. I found it quite difficult to feel relaxed in such a chattering atmosphere. My brother took me further round the corridor and dropped me off at the classroom where he said I had to go. I duly entered the room to be met by other boys that were milling around, waiting to decide at what seat and desk they would be sitting. Very shortly afterwards, a teacher came into the room and asked us all to sit down. Fortunately I managed to sit at a desk that was adjacent to the window that looked out on to the main corridor, so I did not feel quite so shut in, as I would had I been sitting in one of the middle rows of desks. The day went without incident and I do not recall seeing any angel presence at all during that first day at school.

On my way home from school, while sitting on the bus, I was thinking about how enjoyable that first day was and how the angels were right; I had no need to be scared at all. Most of the other boys seemed quite friendly and the nerves that we all had seemed to disappear relatively quickly during that first morning.

The weeks went by with normal school activity and I was enjoying all of the lessons. I was very good at mathematics and also performed quite well at English language and English literature. I also enjoyed some of the newer subjects that were not taught at junior school; for example, I enjoyed science and in particular chemistry. I was very, very excited about the history subjects being taught and I also quite liked geography and learning to communicate in French. I was not necessarily the most academic of pupils during the first couple of years of grammar school, but was in the middle-to-top streams in most of the subjects.

I continued to see the angels Chrystal and Bellina on an ongoing basis throughout the months and early years of being at grammar school and most of the chats we had centred on normal day-to-day activities, talking about some of the family issues that I faced and also some of the school issues that cropped up occasionally. I also regularly saw other children's guardian angels during some of the lessons at school, and in particular during periods of play out in the playground, which for Northern Grammar School was called the quadrangle, as the play area was right in the middle of the four sides of the school building. The actual building was square-shaped and the concreted play area was in the middle of this. It became abundantly clear to me that the angels really enjoyed playtime, as it gave them the opportunity to really connect with each of the children. If you go past any school playground, especially infant and junior schools, when they are at play, you can hear the excited voices of the children bellowing out as they run around and play their games, full of naivety and excitement. I can assure you that the angels love this time to be with the children in such a carefree, relaxed and happy way. If only we in adulthood could recapture and retain some of that joyful enthusiasm, I am sure all of our lives would be that much better.

It was in my second year of senior school when something momentous happened that I could not at the time understand. It was during a history lesson. The teacher was standing at the blackboard and he had written something on the blackboard with chalk. He commented on some of the things he had written; I think it was about 1066 and the Battle of Hastings. When he had finished talking about that particular subject, he turned back to the board and started to erase the writing on the blackboard with an old-fashioned chalk eraser. The sun shone in through the classroom window and I could see all of the chalk dust billowing out as he was cleaning the blackboard, and this dust was floating in the rays of the sun. I then saw the most beautiful and incredible thing.

Literally out of the rays of sunlight and chalk dust, a gentleman appeared. This man walked behind the teacher and faced the class; he was as real as you and me. I looked around at the other children's faces to see what they thought and to see if any of them were commenting on this person that had just appeared. To my amazement, not one of the children had seen this man appear, there was no excitement on their faces; they were all just looking at the teacher, who had just finished rubbing out the writing on the blackboard. The teacher then went on to talk about a different subject, but I sat transfixed, with my eyes on the other man.

He was about five foot ten inches tall, had short dark hair, and was wearing a black suit, white shirt, black tie and shiny black shoes. He looked straight at me and said, 'You can see me, can't you?'

I did not know what to say, but I blurted out, 'Yes.' With that, the boy who I was sat next to looked at me strangely.

The teacher shouted across to me, 'Woolley, what did you say?' (The teachers often referred to us by our surnames.)

I did not answer as I was still looking at the other man in the room. The teacher repeated, 'Woolley, what did you say?'

I replied, 'I didn't say anything.'

The teacher said, 'You shouted something out – what was it?'

At that stage I was so afraid, I thought I had better tell the truth and I said that I had said 'yes'.

It was at this stage that it became abundantly clear to me that neither the teacher nor any of the other boys could see this person. The teacher then said that I would have a one-hour detention for shouting out during lessons. The teacher then continued with the lesson.

The other man, who was obviously a spirit, was still standing next to the teacher during all of this. He again said to me, 'You can see me, can't you? I am sorry that I just got you into trouble – I did not mean for that to happen.'

I did not know what to do or say; the one certainty was I could not say anything out loud as that would have incurred further trouble with the teacher. I tried to communicate via thought, which I found so easy to do with the angels, but for whatever reason this spirit did not seem to pick up on my thought. He kept talking to me. I could hear him clearly and all other voices in the room at this point faded into the background, whereas the spirit carried on talking and was speaking clearly and eloquently. He kept asking me questions like what was my name, how often I had seen spirits, had I been taught any of this, did I know what to do with this gift, did I know what would happen to me next, and so on? I just sat there transfixed, listening to him talk. He said to me that he often visited the school as he had many happy memories of it himself. He said to me to enjoy my day and that I may well be meeting him again. With that, he just turned and faced the blackboard and literally took one step towards it and totally vanished. Fortunately, shortly after that the lesson ended.

Some of the other boys that I had become a little closer to during the first year or so at school came over to me to ask why I had shouted out in the class. I really did not know what to say and just mumbled something to the effect that I didn't know. I felt that I couldn't say anything without opening myself up to be ridiculed. The last time I had mentioned something like this to a teacher was in junior school, about seeing angels. I got into trouble with both my teacher and parents and was told that I would get into further trouble if I ever mentioned anything like this again.

Looking back, I think the reason this spirit took me by surprise was because my previous connections with the spirit world had mainly consisted of contact with angels and I had tended to treat the angels as an everyday part of my life. Whereas I could tell from the energy and some of the things that this spirit said, coupled with my inability to be able to communicate with him through thought, that this spirit was indeed different. For the rest of that day, I felt a little uneasy and even slightly unwell. In fact, some of my friends on that day said to me I looked quite white and shaken; they thought it was because I managed to get my first detention!

When I went home that night, I went straight to my room and got changed out of my uniform into casual clothes. I was standing looking out of my bedroom window into the garden and suddenly became aware that the angel Chrystal had joined me. I turned to face her and she said that she had come to talk to me about what happened at school that day. I asked her if she had seen what happened.

She smiled and said, 'I always know what happens.'

I sat on the bed and Chrystal sat at the other end and she asked me if I knew who the spirit was and if I could explain the emotions that I had had at the time. I said to her that I had seen the man and he had talked to me, and I had tried to talk back to him, through thought, but he did not hear what I was saying. Chrystal smiled at that and said the angels would one day teach me about earthbound spirits and why they are attracted on occasions to those people showing extra light. I told her that I felt quite unwell after the experience and even now still felt quite tired, listless and unwell. I cannot recall the exact things Chrystal said on this occasion, but she was talking about vibrational changes, energy shifts, and so on. I do recall, however, Chrystal saying to me that when an earthbound spirit comes into contact with a human being, especially in close proximity, then depending on the spirit in question, the earthly body of the human can be adversely affected. Chrystal then said that what I was feeling was a reflection that some of my light and energy had drained away during this meeting, although this was not the spirit's intention, and that I would soon be back to my normal self.

Chrystal said she would help this process straightaway and she asked me to close my eyes. As I did this, I was immediately engulfed in a deep colour green. I felt Chrystal move to stand in front of me and she placed both of her hands on my shoulders. Chrystal asked me to breathe in a relaxed way and to just breathe in the colour green, which I did. I suddenly felt my whole body pulsating and vibrating, as though I was being fuelled with energy. I opened my eyes and was amazed to see that Chrystal was still at the other end of the bed, sitting there, and another angel was in the room also. It was this angel that had actually put her hands on my shoulders. The love, warmth and energy from this angel was out of this world, literally!

Angel Chrystal immediately knew what I was thinking and she told me to enjoy the feeling I was experiencing and that this was a deep healing session that the angels were giving me. Chrystal also told me the name of the angel that had given me the healing, but sadly I am unable to recall it. Chrystal said the angel in question worked very closely with another archangel called Raphael. Chrystal said she had asked Archangel Raphael to send this angel of healing to restore my vitality after the incident with the spirit earlier that day. I must have sat there for at least twenty minutes blissfully absorbing all of the wonderful feelings that I was receiving. It concluded with the healing angel stepping back from me, removing her hands from my shoulders, and I will always remember her words, 'Bless you, my child.' I could feel tears in my eyes as I felt the release and relief surging through my body. Angel Chrystal said she would leave me now and let me recover in peace.

I continued to do quite well at school for the first couple of years, despite feeling different from all the other boys. I maintained the position of being in the medium-to-top groups in all the subjects I was taking. I also excelled at athletics and represented the school in the triple jump. I particularly remember one amusing incident while preparing at Alexandra Park athletics track for an inter-schools competition. I was warming up around the track on my own and decided to just jog round the full 400-metre track to loosen up, prior to my event taking place that afternoon. I was halfway around the track when I suddenly noticed that I had been joined by two angels on my right-hand side. These were angels that I had never seen before. They were both about eight feet tall and had the most remarkable wings and long flowing dresses. As is the norm when I see angels presenting themselves in that way, I could not see their feet or any contact of them touching the floor; they just seemed to be gliding along next to me.

I was jogging along very slowly and turned to look to my right and said to the angels, 'Are you here to help me or to race me?'

They both chuckled at this and replied by saying, 'We can race you if you like.'

I thought this would be quite good fun and started to speed up to a more medium pace and said to the angels, 'Catch me if you can.'

Without any effort they were just gliding alongside me and as we turned round into the final bend, about one hundred metres or so from the finish line, I said to the angels, 'I will really go for it now and let's see how fast you are.'

At this point, I started to sprint to the finish line. Much to my amusement, and obviously theirs as well, as I was running full pelt, I looked ahead of me to the winning line, which was still some ninety metres or so to go, and both angels were standing by the winning line, looking at me running at full speed towards them. I continued to run as fast as I could and sprinted across the winning line. I then turned to look at both of them and they both had huge smiles across their faces. There were quite a few other people milling around at this time, so I did not talk out loud, but I immediately sent the thought, 'Hey, you two cheated and should be disqualified.'

I immediately heard a response back from one of them saying, 'We possess the ability to manifest ourselves wherever we would like to be; we will leave the running and the hard work to you!'

I laughed out loud at this, as did both angels.

Later on in my actual event, the triple jump, I took three separate jumps, the second of which was the furthest I had ever jumped, and I finished fifth overall in the competition. I was well pleased with that, although if I could have had just a little bit of the angels' power of being able to manifest myself further up the sandpit, I could have added at least another couple of metres on!

Life at home was still quite tough, and in 1967 my father finished the last of his main jobs as a welfare ambulance driver. From that moment on, other than when he was well enough to take on the odd short-term job, he became more and more physically ill and also suffered with severe depression. My mother had taken up a house-cleaning position to supplement the family income. My mother was still obviously looking after all of us, even though we were all over ten years old, but the hours that she spent at work coupled with looking after the family was made increasingly difficult by my father's ill health. While my parents had enough money to get by on what my mother earned, along with any pension or benefits my father was receiving, times were still tough. I do not recall any major luxuries as a child, although both my parents tried very hard to give us all they could. Certainly at Christmas time there was very limited money available for my parents and they must have struggled tremendously in buying just the odd present that we did have, like an Action Man figure, fruit and nuts and the odd chocolate selection box. We always had a Christmas tree and decorations up, and even though there was no money for any presents of any note, I still feel that the tradition of Christmas was upheld much more in those days, as opposed to the commercial realities that now seem to beset Christmas.

I have a stark recollection of an awful event that happened in our house in Orchard Road when I was about twelve. My younger sister Karen would have been about seven and a half at the time and she had obviously done something naughty or something to upset my father. I was upstairs and I heard him shouting and screaming at her. I went to the top of the stairs and could hear him smacking her and shouting at her. Karen was crying uncontrollably. I have no idea what she did – perhaps she did very little and this was one of those incidents when my father just snapped – but whatever caused it, the following events were very traumatic.

My father continued to smack Karen and shout at her and he was beginning to push her towards the cellar door. He opened the cellar door and said she could go down there. Karen was terrified of this and was by now getting hysterical. I started to come down the stairs and shouted to my father to not put Karen down the cellar, knowing full well how terrifying that can be. He shouted at me to go back up the stairs and I heard him push Karen into the cellar and lock the door behind her. It was very dark in there and I have no knowledge if Karen even knew where the light was. It would have been very dangerous to have tried to walk down the stairs into the cellar without the light on, and Karen may well have just sat on the step the other side of the door. I could hear her crying and sobbing uncontrollably, however, and my father went back into the dining room to watch the television.

I felt enormous pains of sorrow for Karen, and I was desperate to open the door and let her out, but I knew I could not do that otherwise I would incur my father's wrath as well. I ran back to my bedroom, and pleaded with the angels to come to me immediately. Angel Bellina immediately arrived and said the angels were well aware of what had happened and they would automatically go to Karen to try to provide her with some comfort and support.

I could still hear Karen, who was by now quite traumatised and hysterical, in the dark of the cellar. I said to Bellina that I could not stand to hear the torment and sorrow of my sister anymore and I pleaded with them to do something to immediately stop this. Bellina said that this was one of life's many lessons, and all I could do in those circumstances was to send positive, loving thoughts to the situation. I was very cross with Bellina for saying this, and there was no way I was just going to sit there and try to send loving thoughts to what she called 'the situation'. I asked Bellina, if the angels were that powerful, why did they let these things happen, and why couldn't they stop it. Bellina was as sensitive and as caring as ever as she tenderly said to me that human free will will always be the driving force for what happens on earth and the angels would try to influence as much as possible, but they could not intervene to prevent some of these things happening. I did not understand this to any degree at the time and was still very cross that the angels did not do anything to try to stop my sister's obvious suffering.

At that stage, my main guardian angel, Chrystal, arrived and Bellina stayed in the room also. Chrystal said that she had been talking to my father's guardian angel and that the angels would try to influence my father's thoughts to soften the situation. I thought this was a very strange thing to say as I could not understand why Chrystal did not go to my father and talk to him directly, but obviously I now know better.

Something must have happened, because shortly after that I heard my father go to the cellar door, unlock it and open it and say to Karen, 'Right, you can come out now,' and he then went back to watch the television. Karen emerged from the cellar and went straight to her bedroom. I said nothing to Karen at the time, and indeed have said nothing to her since, but I am grateful that the angels brought to a swift conclusion the obvious distress that she was feeling.

Chrystal and Bellina stayed with me for at least another hour, talking to me about the emotions I had felt on behalf of another. Bellina asked me to describe my feelings and to say exactly where in my body I was having them. I said to her that it broke my heart to hear Karen crying so uncontrollably and I also found myself powerless and useless in trying to prevent what was happening to her. I said that I wished I could have traded places with her and taken on her suffering, rather than her having to go through this ordeal. I had faced many previous instances myself, and as a child I had developed the ability to mentally switch myself off from some of the suffering that I faced on similar occasions.

Bellina asked me why I would have wanted to change places with Karen; having experienced many such instances myself, why would I have wanted to put myself into that position. I said to her that the pain and hurt I felt for Karen's suffering was greater than the pain and hurt I felt for myself. Both Chrystal and Bellina came closer to me at that stage and put their loving arms around me. I could sense and see their beautiful angel wings engulfing us all; it was almost as though the three of us were entwined together within their wings. Bellina said the lesson that I had learnt at that stage was to feel empathy for others, to actually feel what they were feeling. She said that when I performed healing in later life, this empathy and sensitivity would stand me in good stead to understand the type of healing that was required. I was emotionally drained at the end of my talk with them both and they laid me down on the bed and asked me to close my eyes, and I could feel them drifting away simultaneously as I was falling asleep.

By the time I had got to year three at grammar school, I began to develop closer friendships with my classmates. In particular, I became very close to a boy called Ian Smith and two others, whose names were Steven Fisher and Stephen Wringe. I was very close to all three of them throughout my remaining years at school. I used to see all three of the boys outside of school, visiting them at their homes for tea, and so on. I have no recollection of any of the three coming to my house, but I certainly recall going to theirs.

Ian had the most amazing guardian angel, who was an angel of extreme size but also extreme power. He reminded me very much of Archangel Michael with his strong presence. On many occasions when I was out with Ian, my guardian angel Chrystal and his used to walk side by side with us. I used to wonder why Ian had a male guardian angel and I had such a feminine, female guardian angel. I can only assume it was the energy that both of us needed at that time. Both the other boys had guardian angels that were very keen to present themselves on many occasions, with Steven Fisher's guardian angel being very similar to himself. I remember Steven as being of slight build with blond hair and his guardian angel looked the same, but obviously much taller. Stephen Wringe had a guardian angel that also had blonde hair and she always spoke in a very practical way. Whereas most guardian angels seem to speak in a soft, sensitive and flowing nature, Stephen's guardian angel spoke in a much more direct and practical way and I used to hear her talking to him constantly, giving practical advice on whatever the issues were facing him at the time.

I used to spend what seemed like hours in their company, listening to their guardian angels talking to them, and I find it incredible that the angels speak with such clarity and yet the human being does not seem to hear any of the comments being made to them at an outward level. Obviously the angels try to communicate in a wide variety of ways, but it did seem strange to me that they could be talking so much without the human they are constantly with paying any attention to them. I was so concerned at this one evening that when I was at home, I went into my bedroom and Angel Chrystal was already there waiting for me.

She said, 'Sit down, Robert, I know you have many questions that you want to ask, and it is now that we feel you are ready to hear some of the answers.'

I immediately told her my thought regarding Stephen Wringe and his guardian angel, whereby Stephen just did not seem to hear or follow any of the advice given by the angel. Chrystal asked me to sit in a more relaxed way, to close my eyes and just listen intently to what she had to say. I cannot remember her words verbatim, but the general gist of what she said was that God, the creator of all, sends angels to earth to be with every living being as a direct messenger from the divine.

She said we were all a part of the divine and that the God light is within all of us. Chrystal said that when we incarnate on earth, we often forget our divine nature and that we get caught up in our earthly woes and worries. She said the angels come to us as a permanent bridge between the issues that we face on earth and the energy and light of the creator. The angels will always be with us and our own personal guardian angel has been with us for this lifetime and all our lifetimes before. She said to me that in later years the angels would fully explain the difference between guardian angels and spirit guides. I do recall her saying that a guardian angel is with us for this lifetime, previous and future lifetimes, whereas a spirit guide comes into our life generally for that one lifetime only, and that for different parts of our life, different spirit guides will come and go. So in essence, the guardian angel is permanently with us and spirit guides are much more of a fluctuating 'in and out' basis.

I asked Chrystal why the angels continue to talk to people that don't hear them. I said that of all the people that I knew at school, I seemed to be the only one that had seen and spoken to the angels and heard what they said back.

Chrystal smiled at this and said the angels use many communication methods. She said they talk to us, send us thoughts, feelings, ideas, images, pictures and that deep inner knowing, along with the wonderful sounds and sights of nature, and that this was just the tip of a very large iceberg. She asked me not to fret over this and said all of this would be explained in later life.

I reiterated what I had said previously, however, and said that I still could not understand why an angel would stand next to somebody and talk continuously with the human being not having any knowledge of the angel's presence. Chrystal said on many occasions the human does not outwardly pick up any message from the angels at that stage, but that the seed is planted and that sometimes over the weeks, months and years ahead this seed would grow and the human would begin to understand some of the angel's input.

I found this all rather strange, but I accepted it at face value. Chrystal said that she did not want to say too much more as I could only take so much in at that stage and that all of the things that I needed to know would be revealed to me at the appropriate time. Chrystal then put her hands on my forehead and I felt this loving warm energy flow through me as she started to fade away.

The very next day at school a new boy started. A couple of boys told me that they thought the new boy was mad and that he was carrying an alien around. I was absolutely fascinated by this thought, so in the lunch period I made a point of going over into the corner of the quadrangle where this boy was. At this time, he was being harassed by another couple of boys from the school. These two were shouting and demanding that the new boy show them the alien he spoke of. Eventually the two boys got fed up and walked off in a huff when the new boy failed to show them anything. I then spoke to this boy and asked him if he would be kind enough to tell me some of the things he had told the other boys. He was reluctant to do so, understandably, so I decided not to push him too much further, but I just told him I would like to be a friend of his. He smiled at me as we parted company. Bellina immediately came to my side and commented that what I had said was very sweet and very supportive, and at a later time more would be revealed to me.

Over the next few weeks, I made a particular point of seeing this boy out in the quadrangle and sports ground as often as possible. He started to open up a bit and started to tell me a bit about himself. I never could find out anything about his family circumstances or what other school he had come from, and it was obvious that he had secrets. On one particular day I was standing with this boy and Angel Chrystal was standing to my side and I saw an angel standing next to the boy. She was the most beautiful sight; she had red hair and an almost burning flame-orange aura. She was certainly a guardian angel, the like of which I had not seen before.

The boy told me that he had a being from another planet that he carried around. I asked him what he meant by saying a 'being from another planet'. He said it was an extraterrestrial. I was really excited by this and felt the deep urge to ask him more. I asked where he had come across this being and whether I could see it. In all of the months ahead, the boy never once told me where he came across this being, if indeed he had one. But he did say he called it Little Aggy. I said to him that was a rather strange name for the being and he just laughed and said, 'That is his name, so that is what I call him.'

I pleaded with him to show me the extraterrestrial, but he constantly refused.

As far as all the other boys in the school were concerned, this boy was mad. Not one person I spoke to had any belief in what the boy had said and certainly, as he never showed anybody anything, it was hard to believe that. All I could say with any great degree of certainty and fact was that this boy had a guardian angel, just like I did and everyone does, and even though his guardian angel appeared different from the majority I had seen, and appeared to be very fiery in substance, this did not in any way disprove what this boy said and maintained about this being.

While everybody else in the school thought he was a fool and did not believe a word he said, I like to believe that everything he said was true. It was just perhaps beyond our comprehension. Now that comment of mine is not based on any factual input and it could be perceived as just wishful thinking on my part. But I had a longing to believe this new boy and he had such unwavering belief in what he said and such courage to keep saying this against extreme adversity, alienating himself totally from the other boys, that I like to believe what he said was true.

When I went home that night, I rushed into the house, hoping that Chrystal or Bellina would be present so that I could talk to them about this. I was very disappointed when I ran to the bedroom and asked for them to come to me to talk and neither appeared. Later on that evening, just before going to bed, I went down to the cellar to play darts. On some occasions, I felt quite strong and courageous enough to go down there, but there were many other times I could not even bring myself to open the door. On this particular evening, I was standing in the cellar playing darts on my own, when suddenly I became aware of the trio of angels appearing, this time in front of me on my left-hand side. Amhiel, Bellina and Chrystal appeared. As usual, Amhiel was in the middle but this time he seemed to be standing further forward than the other two. Amhiel said to me that I had learnt a very important fundamental lesson that day in listening to the boy's story and taking it at face value. He told me that, while all the other boys in the school were judging the new boy and his story of 'the being', he said he was pleased that I had an open mind and was encouraging this boy to talk freely. I did confess at that stage that this was more to do with my inquisitive nature than about supporting the boy! All three angels laughed at this and said that I should not try to talk myself out of the praise that they were giving me. I smiled at that point. Amhiel said that the boy had spoken freely and from the heart and spoke his truth. He said that whereas the other boys has judged him on their own beliefs, their own values and standards, I had retained that open mind and that this was an important lesson for issues that I would face in the future. Still being in an inquisitive state, I asked Amhiel whether what the boy had said was true. Amhiel said to me that it was the boy's truth and that was all that mattered. I thought that this was a very strange answer and I asked Amhiel again, 'But is it the truth?' Amhiel just reiterated what he had said previously. To this day I still do not know what Amhiel meant by his words, but I decided to take that at face value, too.

Amhiel also said to me that he could feel that while I was in the angels' presence in the cellar, I was not exhibiting any signs of any fear or apprehension of being in that environment, whereas on many occasions the angels could sense that I could not even approach the cellar door, let alone go down the stairs. I said to Amhiel that I fully accepted that as being the truth, and I did not know myself why on some days I could go down there and on others could not even bear to be near the door, let alone open it. Amhiel said that that indeed was another lesson that I was shortly to learn: the need to listen to my own inner voice, as well as that of the angels, and the need to perceive energies around me.

I asked him what he meant by this. I had constantly heard the angels talking about energies, but I was not clear on what they meant. He reminded me of the incident at Northern Grammar School in the first year, when the spirit in the black suit had come into the room and reminded me of how I had felt physically at that time. I remembered that I had felt quite drained and sick following this spirit's visit. Amhiel continued by saying that on some days, when I could not even approach the cellar door, I was almost certainly picking up other energy from other spirits that were down in the cellar at that time. I found all this rather off-putting and I asked Amhiel if he meant there were spirits down in the cellar, other than angels. He said that this was indeed the case on some occasions and I would be given greater understanding of this fact as I grew older. He asked me once again to listen to my own inner voice and if ever I felt afraid to go into the cellar then to listen to that voice and honour it. I asked him what would happen if I felt brave enough to be down in the cellar and yet suddenly was overcome by fear once I was down there.

All three angels laughed at this and said, 'Robert, at this stage of your life, the simplest thing is to call in Archangel Michael to surround you in his protection.' I instantly recalled the lovely feeling I had had previously when I had met Archangel Michael and I could visualise the purple colour that had illuminated my bedroom when he had visited me.

Angel Amhiel told me that Archangel Michael was just a thought away. If I was in the cellar or indeed anywhere else where I felt fear all I had to say by thought was 'Archangel Michael, please come to me now', and that very thought would instantly manifest Archangel Michael at my side, protecting me, loving me. I was greatly encouraged by this and I was also greatly encouraged with the simplicity of the command. As the three angels started to disappear, I recommenced my game of darts, feeling very positive and uplifted from the visit of the trio of angels.

Over the next year or so, I continued to do well at school, although setting no academic records in the process! By this stage, I was fourteen years old and most of the boys at school tried to be friends with some of the girls in the adjacent girls' school. I was a little slow on the uptake on that front and was quite happy to continue with my sporting prowess as opposed to trying to find a girlfriend at the tender age of fourteen.

There was one particular girl, however, that most of the boys in my school year made a beeline for whenever we met in the tuck shop (which was at the back of the school and across the road from both the boys' and girls' schools). This particular girl was called Linda Milne. I remember Linda as being an attractive girl with long dark hair. Most of the boys in my year, and indeed the year above, definitely saw her as ideal girlfriend material. I don't think I personally said more than a couple of words to Linda on any occasion, with most of the other boys acting like bees around a honey pot. The thing I did notice, however, about Linda was her confidence. She would be quite happy talking alone to a group of boys, as if she was holding court, with the boys hanging on her every word. The thing I was most fascinated with was not Linda herself, but the two angels that were invariably with her every time I ever saw her. I did not understand why she always had two angels with her where most other people I had come across generally had one (although occasionally there were two or three others as well).

On one particular day while listening to Linda talking to the boys, Chrystal appeared by my side and whispered in my ear if I noticed how strong a connection Linda had to the two angels she had with her. I said I did, and asked Chrystal by thought, why is this? One was invariably a male and one a female and the vast majority of the time it was the same two angels, although on the odd occasion there was another angel with her as well. Chrystal told me that in simple terms, most people have more than one guardian angel, although generally there is always a primary guardian angel.

Chrystal told me that while she was my primary guardian angel, even though she was part of the trio, Linda had two guardian angels that were invariably with her, but these two angels would generally be doing a different role.

I asked Chrystal what she meant by this. She said that one of the guardian angels would be a guardian angel to prompt Linda into taking certain courses of action and making the correct decision. She said the second one would be much more of a supporting guardian angel and would be there to console Linda in times of crisis or sadness in her life. I immediately saw the connection in what she was saying. In simple terms she was indicating that one of the guardian angels would be prompting Linda to take a particular course of action and if Linda followed that course of action, all would be well in her world, and the other guardian angel would be there to provide support to her if she took a wrong course of action where things did not end up so well.

Chrystal laughed out loud as she could tell from my thoughts that I had realised what she was saying to me. I smiled back and sent Chrystal the thought, 'That sounds pretty easy, then: if we all listen to our angels, we can't go wrong.' Chrystal smiled and nodded.

I continued to reflect on what Chrystal had said about angelic guidance in the weeks ahead, and to think how easy life would be if we all could hear our guardian angels and if we followed their every prompt.

It was shortly after this encounter, however, that some of the more typical teenage problems befell me, or should I say I chose the teenage problem path to follow.

Teenage Rebellion

Around the age of fourteen or fifteen, I started to take up most of the normal things that teenage boys do. For example, I played in a school football team that was called Centurion FC. It would be an understatement to say that the team was not very good. On one particular occasion, we played another youth football team and we lost 51–0. Considering the game itself was only of ninety minutes' duration, it seems remarkable to me now that we could possibly have lost by that score. That is just over a goal every two minutes. That must have gone into some record book somewhere; or the referee could not count!

Most of the Centurion players were between the ages of thirteen and fourteen on average, whereas the teams we were playing seemed to have an average age of sixteen to seventeen. So I think I can safely say that we were outclassed and outmuscled on every front. All of our team did, however, enjoy the games that we played, and even though the team only lasted for about three months before breaking up totally, we were all very sporting players and just enjoyed taking to the football field for the fun and excitement of the game. We certainly did not have the same competitive edge of all the other teams that we played.

It was about this time when I started to go out with some of my friends after school in the early evenings, and do the normal things that boys did at that stage. This mainly consisted of walking about, or going into one of the other boys' houses. At this stage, I tended to rush through my homework as fast as possible in order to go out for a few hours with my friends. I still did the homework that I was given, but perhaps not to the standard that I had been doing it in the preceding three years or so.

On one occasion, I particularly remember rushing through my English and maths homework and putting my completed work back in my schoolbag as fast as possible. As I was getting changed out of my school uniform and into my casual clothes, ready to go out with my friend, Ian Smith, Chrystal suddenly appeared in the far corner of the room. I do not recall now how the conversation started but Chrystal was talking to me and I was responding while still getting changed into my casual clothes.

At one part of the conversation, and I particularly remember this point, Chrystal said to me, 'Robert, why are you not listening to me?'

Chrystal said this in such a tone that I knew that she wanted me to give more attention to what she was saying. By this time, I had just about got dressed and put my training shoes on ready to go out. I said to Chrystal that I was indeed listening to what she was saying (knowing, of course, that I was probably not listening at all).

Chrystal continued by saying that it was good that I now had lots of friends to go out and play with and the angels were pleased to encourage this. She did say, however, that there was a time for everything and that it was important that I also continued to concentrate on my schoolwork. I must say, and I remember this feeling quite clearly, that I felt Chrystal was batting for a lost cause at that particular moment! I was desperately keen to go out and see Ian and some of my other friends as it was a couple of days before Bonfire Night on 5 November, and at school some of the boys had said that they had a few fireworks to bring out with us on that evening. Over the preceding weekend, a couple of them had made a very small bonfire that we could light up. I felt great excitement at the prospect of this, as this would have been the first bonfire or fireworks event that I had attended alone, separate from my parents as a child.

I always had happy memories of this time of year as I remember fondly the times that I used to go out with my handmade guy on my 'penny for the guy' trips. From the ages of around eight to twelve, a couple of weeks before fireworks night, I used to go out with my guy and stand around chosen spots in the Portsmouth area, asking for a penny for the guy. I used to meet some wonderful people doing this, and some very kind people, too. All of the money that I ever obtained carrying out this activity was always put towards Christmas presents for my parents and brother and sisters. At that stage, I never had any interest in fireworks and was pleased to use the money for Christmas presents for others.

Returning now to the conversation I was having with Chrystal, I acknowledged to Chrystal that I fully understood what she said with regard to schoolwork and playtime. I tried to explain and justify the reason that I was so excited about going out with my friends. Chrystal said that we could talk further about this and that I should go out and enjoy myself. Before departing the room, however (and on this occasion I left the room first, rather than Chrystal disappearing), she asked me to remember what she had said regarding the importance of schoolwork and she also supplemented that by asking me to be safe while out with the other boys on that particular evening, I took this advice in a rather glib fashion and said to Chrystal I would see her later as I exited the bedroom.

I excitedly ran all the way to Ian's house, which was about a mile and a half away from mine. At this stage of my life, I seemed to have the capacity to run for ever without getting excessively tired. Ian was awaiting my arrival and standing outside his front door when I reached his house and we set off excitedly to meet the other boys at the prearranged spot near the recreation ground. By the time we arrived at the recreation ground, there were about six or seven other boys, and a couple of girls there, too. We were all of a similar age. We walked off as a group to an area of disused wasteland where the small bonfire had been prepared a few days earlier. By the time we got there, it was already getting much darker and it was a clear evening, although a little cold. We were standing around the bonfire, which at this stage was not lit, when one of the girls opened a carrier bag that she had been carrying. She said that her mother had made some toffee and fudge for all of us.

She proceeded to break up bits of toffee to give to us individually, and a couple of pieces of fudge, too. I must say her mother must have been a good cook because it tasted lovely. One of the other boys then decided to light the bonfire and produced a box of matches to do this. It took at least six or seven goes to get the bonfire to light, but eventually some of the smaller twigs did catch fire and the small bonfire that had been prepared let out a beautiful orange glow as the flames took hold of some of the bigger bits of wood. The actual wooden structure of the fire was only about five feet high but the flames seemed to shoot up at least another three feet higher than that. We all stood around the bonfire, feeling the wonderful heat and glow that it was giving off. My friends and I were fairly well-behaved children, as were the other boys and girls we were with that night, and the bonfire was built in a very safe place and it was of no hazard to the surrounding area.

One of the other boys then produced the fireworks that he had managed to obtain. He had about four rockets, ten bangers, as they were called in those days, and a couple of Catherine wheels. We found a couple of milk bottles to rest the rockets in and there were some wooden posts around on a metal perimeter fence, into which we hammered some old nails that we had found lying around on the floor so that we could put the Catherine wheels up on the posts. The rockets were duly lit and they each let out an enormous screech as they were fired into the night sky. Standing relatively close to the rockets, I instantly thought of what Chrystal had said regarding safety. I must admit it was at this particular point that I realised the sheer ferocity that some of these fireworks had, even in those days. I was pleased that I did not personally light any of the rockets or Catherine wheels or indeed any of the bangers, as I was quite happy just standing back watching the mini display.

The bonfire itself can only have lasted an hour or so before it petered out with no direct flames but its simmering embers were still red hot. At this stage, we all walked back to the recreation ground and stood around chatting for another thirty minutes or so before dispersing as a group to all make our own way home. I walked with Ian as I passed his house anyway on the way back to mine. I said cheerio to him at his front door and I then jogged home. I had a brief chat and something to eat with the rest of the family before going to bed.

I was lying in bed, drifting off slowly to sleep, when I became acutely aware of the bedroom being lit up by a golden light. I felt that Chrystal had reappeared and I opened my eyes and sat up and saw the trio of angels had once again arrived. On this occasion,

Amhiel and Chrystal said nothing in particular but Bellina took a step forward from the other two angels and asked me if I had enjoyed myself earlier that evening. I said I had, and that it was great fun to see the bonfire be lit and to feel the warmth of the glow throughout my entire body. I said to her I was quite surprised as to how hot the bonfire got, as even though I was standing about six to eight feet away from the bonfire itself, I could feel the heat on the skin of my face. I also said that I enjoyed watching the fireworks, albeit from a bit of a distance.

Bellina said that I had learnt another lesson earlier that evening, even if I was not conscious of it. She said it was important to have fun by all means, and to enjoy occasions like the one I had experienced earlier that evening, but she took the opportunity to stress once again the need for safety in situations such as that. I said that I had been totally safe and stood well back from the bonfire itself and had not even lit any of the fireworks. She said the important lesson I had learnt, even if I was not conscious of this, was that I needed to honour myself and to go with my own feelings. She said there would be occasions later on in my teenage years when I would be goaded by other children to do certain things. She said it was very important to go with my inner feelings (which I now know some people call a sixth sense or gut instinct) and to only do what was right for me. She said as I got older I would understand that the pressure of a group, or peer pressure, often got people into dangerous and difficult situations. She said if I honoured myself and honoured what I knew to be right on all occasions, no harm would come to me.

I said thank you to Bellina for this, knowing her words to be right. Just before Bellina stepped back to be more in line with Amhiel and Chrystal, she asked me something that at the time I thought was very odd. She said to me that when I talked to Amhiel and Chrystal, I used their name frequently but when I talked to her I did not refer to her by her name. I laughed at this and said I was not sure why this was so but it might be something to do with the fact that I often had difficulty in pronouncing the name Bellina, whereas Amhiel and Chrystal just seemed to roll off the tongue.

She said that she had picked up by thought the name that I

used to call her in my head when I was thinking of the trio of angels. I immediately blurted out the name Bella. She reminded me that angels operate on a vibration basis and they were happy to use whatever name suited me the best. She said that she would be delighted if I called her Bella, which anyway had a very close vibration to her full name of Bellina.

I thanked Bellina for this and said, 'Right, from now on then I will call you Bella.'

I also looked at Chrystal and Amhiel and all three angels were smiling.

Amhiel then said he had some important things to talk to me about. He said that I had been seeing the trio of angels ever since my earliest childhood memories and that I now fully understood what their differing roles were.

I thought Amhiel was going to check to see if I remembered what their roles were and excitedly said, 'Amhiel, I know you are here to protect me, and I know Chrystal is here to guide me and prompt me, and I know Bella is here to comfort me and support me.'

I was pleased with myself in saying those words so quickly in response to what Amhiel was saying. Amhiel laughed at this point and said to me he was not going to ask that at all. This was clearly an occasion when I pre-guessed what the angels were about to say and got it totally wrong!

Amhiel said, 'No, Robert, I am here to teach you some more fundamental things about angels.'

Amhiel continued by saying that they had manifested themselves to me in my childhood years in the form many humans like to see them. He said, for example, that when they had shown themselves to me they invariably showed themselves with their beautiful light, their flowing robes and their majestic angel wings.

He said angels had presented themselves in this way for thousands of years, in earth time, because that is the way that the humans gained great comfort in seeing angels, and also because it differentiates them from other spiritual beings. He did say, however, that their true form is one of light. Amhiel said that they had no physical substance like we do on earth and they can manifest themselves in whatever way they choose at the time.

They can do this by having a haze of light, an orb of light or even in their majestic 'eight foot tall with wings' presentation.

Amhiel also said, and at the time I found this very confusing, 'Robert, we also manifest ourselves in human form on occasions so that we can mingle with you without your knowledge that we are here.'

I asked Amhiel what he meant by this and he said on some occasions the angels appear just as any other human being looks. He said sometimes an angel would be wearing a suit and tie and would have normal earthly shoes on and be walking around in a high street without anybody knowing that was an angel. He also said they could be wearing just a normal dress and look like any other woman walking down the high street. When he gave his third illustration of this fact, I must admit it touched my heart. He said on some occasions the angel manifests itself as a beggar in the street, somebody sitting there in human form, looking totally dishevelled and dirty.

He said the angels only ever did this on very rare occasions and I asked him why they would possibly do that. He said when an angel presents itself in this form, they could be, for example, sitting in a doorway, looking totally alienated from the rest of the human race. He said the vast majority of the population would just walk past any such person sitting in a shop doorway looking like that, but he said occasionally, and it was very occasionally, somebody would walk past and look at this poor person sitting in a doorway. He said eye contact would be made between the two, and the person walking by may stop and take a small amount of change out of their pocket or purse, and give it to the person in the doorway. He said a deep loving eye contact would be made between these two and the person would carry on walking up the high street after having given their small donation of change, feeling illuminated and generally feeling good about giving.

Amhiel said this was an occasion of somebody giving from their heart and, even if it was only a few pence, the money would have been gratefully received from any such person in a doorway. He said the act of kindness itself far exceeded the monetary value of the exchange. He said this act of giving would have been purely from the heart and would have provided a soul-to-soul connection between the angel and the person. He said the love behind the giving gesture was immeasurable, and far exceeded any monetary value possible. I must admit I was very touched by the way Amhiel was putting this short story across to me. I asked Amhiel how would we know if ever we saw an angel in human form in such circumstances or even totally different circumstances. He looked at me intently and said, 'You wouldn't know.' I thought this was a very telling comment.

Amhiel finished some of the things he was saying by indicating that on some occasions he himself, and Chrystal and Bella, may well present themselves to me in human form, as opposed to angelic form with wings and so on, but that I would know it was them on every occasion.

I said I would be quite happy to see any of the trio of angels in whatever form they wanted to present themselves, as I always felt uplifted by their comments and their presence. Just before the trio of angels departed, Chrystal said to me that while in my younger years the angels had told me about something that I would later refer to as the four clairs, they would also develop in me the ability to be able to teach others how they could also have a much better contact with the angelic realms.

Chrystal said most human beings measure their ability to see anything of a spiritual nature with external eyes only. She said that while the gift of normal sight was obviously important, the gift of full clairvoyant sight was also important for those wishing to follow a spiritual path. At this stage, I recalled some of the previous things the angels had said to me, in relation to how people could develop their clairvoyant sight should they wish to do so, as well as developing the other senses which were of equal importance regarding the ability to hear angels, sense angels and pick up on the many thoughts and ideas that angels continually give us.

Chrystal told me that the angels were fully aware that I was taking all of my contact and interaction with them as just a normal day-to-day activity, and that they had been quite happy to allow this to continue in this vein. She did say, however, that in later life I would fully value the unique gift that had been bestowed upon me and the reasons behind that, when compared to many other people either on a spiritual path and seeking to develop their abilities or even those not on any spiritual path at all. Chrystal said that my contact with the angels had been thorough and ongoing and it would continue to be at that level, and that when the time was right I was to talk openly and freely of this, which would act as a catalyst for many others to follow the path into the wonderful world of angels.

The angels then said that they would be leaving me now as I was getting very tired and I needed to get my sleep, and with that the angels turned and vanished.

It must have been a couple of months later when I was in one of my school lessons – and this time it was a science lesson – that once again I saw the spirit of the gentleman that I had seen previously during a history class. The teacher was walking around the class handing out homework that he had marked previously. While the teacher was walking round, I looked up towards the front of the class and saw the spirit standing there by the teacher's desk. He said out loud, 'You can still see me, can't you?'

After having got a detention the last time I answered this spirit out loud, I just answered by thought, saying, 'Yes, I can still see you.'

This time the spirit seemed to hear me clearly because he continued to speak out loud in response to any answers I provided by thought.

He said to me, 'Why is it that only you can see me and none of the others boys can?' I sent a thought back to him saying I did not know the answer to that. He said something that I thought was quite humorous when he then said, 'This teacher thinks he is so clever but even he can't see me.'

I smiled at that. The spirit said he visited the school on occasions for the reasons that he had told me during his earlier visit when he said that he had many happy memories of the school.

This time I decided to ask some direct questions myself. I asked him why he had happy memories of the school and he said out loud, 'That is obvious – because I also used to be a boy at this school.' I asked him if he knew any of the teachers, and he said he knew some of the teachers and also the headmaster, but that some of the other teachers were new to him. I asked him how he got into the school when he decided to visit, and he said whenever he thought of the school, he just found himself to be in a classroom. I then asked something, which looking back was probably quite a good question to ask – where he was when he was not in the school.

He said, 'I generally just walk around and go to other places I know.'

At this stage I really wished I had asked him his name, but at no stage did it ever cross my mind to ask this question. The spirit became a little agitated at this point and I could sense that he was feeling uneasy. He kept saying, 'Why can't any of these other boys hear me? Why doesn't this teacher hear me? Why is it only you that can see me? Why is it that I can hear what you say to me even though your mouth isn't moving?'

He appeared very restless and started to pace around at the front of the class.

Fortunately, on this occasion, I felt quite strong during the exchange with this spirit and I didn't feel drained in any shape or form whatsoever. What I did not realise at the time was, while some of the latter exchange was going on with this spirit, the science teacher must have been talking to me because I was suddenly aware of him standing by me when he slapped a large ruler on my desk, which made an almighty cracking sound. I turned to the left to look at the science teacher, who was shouting at me for not answering his questions. I had absolutely no knowledge of the science teacher talking to me during my exchange with the spirit, but obviously he must have been. All of the other boys were looking in my direction, amazed that I was saying nothing in response to the teacher's questions.

The teacher continued by saying to me that I would be getting a 'conduct mark' for not answering him when he was speaking to me. I rather limply apologised at this point and said sorry for not answering but I could not hear what he was saying. The science teacher turned his back on me, as he was walking to the front of the class, and said, 'Woolley, you need to get your ears tested.'

At least on this occasion I did not get a detention!

I normally caught a bus home from school, but on one particular day, a few weeks later, I decided to walk home. I think I had spent the bus fare money on some sweets in the school tuck shop at lunchtime.

Anyway, while walking home I was suddenly aware that I had an angelic presence on my right-hand side, walking alongside me. I turned to my right to look and there, standing to my right, walking right along next to me, was the angel Chrystal. This time, however, while Chrystal looked to all intents and purposes as she normally does, in respect of her long flowing blonde hair, beautiful face and so on, I was aware that she had a long flowing dress on, and this time was not showing any angel wings at all. In fact, she looked similar to many other women that you would see walking about if they were dressed in a similar vein. The major difference, however, was that while Chrystal was dressed in a long, flowing dress that other women could easily wear, there was a considerable aura around Chrystal, which was golden in colour, and even though she was walking alongside me, she still appeared to float. This time I could clearly see Chrystal had feet with shoes on and was walking as anyone else would walk. I was really pleased to see Chrystal because it was at least going to be an hours' walk home and I would enjoy the time much more talking to Chrystal en route. Ever since I had seen the spirit in the classroom, in the science lesson, I had been thinking on and off about what he was doing there, so I decided to ask Chrystal for her views.

Rather surprisingly, rather than giving me any straight answers to the questions I posed, Chrystal asked me for my interpretation as to the reasons the spirit came to the school. I said to Chrystal I had no idea why I had seen this particular spirit on two occasions, and other than knowing that the spirit, while in human form, had attended the school, I had no idea why he presented himself back there. Chrystal asked me to think as to the potential reason why he came back. I clearly remember saying that the man obviously enjoyed his time at the school while he was a boy and I presume it was purely to experience the good memories that he had.

I was obviously not doing very well in my answers because Chrystal started to prompt me with further questions. She asked me why I thought that the spirit was getting a little bit agitated when he was asking why nobody else in the class saw him. I really did not know the answer to that question. Chrystal also asked me to remember what the spirit had said about where he used to go when he was not visiting the school. I definitely remember that one. I told Chrystal that the spirit had said that he used to walk around or go to other places that he knew. I think Chrystal could clearly see that I was struggling to answer many of her more direct questions and I presume it was that which prompted her to tell me the following.

She said that the spirit in question was what many people refer to as an earthbound spirit. She told me that this spirit was a young gentleman that had been involved in a road traffic accident, which unfortunately had resulted in his death. She said that, for whatever reason, in this particular case, the spirit had not moved fully over to the spirit world upon his untimely death. She said that this happened on occasions and is best described as the spirit not passing over to the light. She said that in the vast majority of cases when human beings die, their spirit releases and passes over to the light. In this particular instance, however, for whatever reason, the spirit did not go to the light and became what Chrystal referred to as earthbound.

She said that occasionally when this happened, the spirit almost does not know that the human body has died and remains in an 'iterative loop', visiting places where they have strong emotional links, and in this particular case that emotional link made the spirit manifest himself at the school.

Chrystal also said that on occasions spirits would manifest themselves to mediums and suchlike, because they were exhibiting light that the spirit was attracted to. I asked Chrystal if this is what the old-fashioned films show when they have séances. Chrystal smiled and said, 'Well, yes, that is something similar.'

I continued by asking Chrystal whether the spirit would just keep visiting the school for ever and ever. She said that was possible in some respects, although she would hope that before too long the spirit would be rescued. I was a little taken aback by that comment and asked Chrystal why the spirit would need to be rescued when he was quite happy to visit the school with all of its happy memories. Chrystal said that the angels would teach me a lot in the next few years regarding spiritual evolution and the actions that need to be taken in order to evolve spirits to their next level.

This was a little beyond me but I accepted what Chrystal said. She said that I would be active in something that she called 'spirit rescue' and she said that this spirit that had visited the school was a classic example of an earthbound spirit that would benefit greatly from being passed over to the light. She said I would carry out many such spirit rescues.

I asked Chrystal whether or not the angels could help this particular spirit, if indeed he did need to be rescued, especially now that they knew that he used to visit the school. Chrystal smiled at that and said that the spirit itself also needed to be ready to move over to the light and could not in essence be forced to move into the light. I was more than a little surprised by that comment. Chrystal concluded this part of the conversation by saying that in this particular instance the spirit was indeed a little lost and the angels would help wherever possible. Throughout the remainder of my days at Northern Grammar School, I did not see this spirit again. I hope, therefore, that the angels passed him over to the light and that his spiritual progression is now back on track.

While walking home with Chrystal walking alongside me, I was suddenly conscious of the people that were walking in the opposite direction to Chrystal and me. Many of these people would walk past me and either brush one arm or the other as they passed me, which in essence made some of them 'walk through' Chrystal. I always found this sight rather amazing because I could see Chrystal as clearly as I could any other human being. She seemed to have a physical appearance walking alongside me, yet other people walking in the opposite direction could literally walk straight through her. I did pass the odd person who seemed to look strangely at me and even a couple of people who used to turn round as they were passing me. I wonder to this day whether they were clairvoyant and saw what I could see.

By the time I was fifteen, I really began to enter a more rebellious stage. I was still doing OK at school but had settled in a medium category of academic ability. I think mathematics was the only subject where I was still in the top group. I was quite tall for my age and must have been about six foot at the age of fifteen. From a social perspective, Ian was still my closest friend, although when we used to go out, we also used to mix with boys a couple of years older than us.

It was when we used to go out with these older boys that I realised that receiving just a small amount of pocket money from home in no way funded the life I now wanted to lead. The elder boys that we used to mix with always seemed to have cash on them and could easily go into shops and buy sweets, chocolate and drink and so on, whereas Ian and I hardly ever had any money. The money I did have was earned by doing a paper round every morning prior to school, and at weekends. I used to quite enjoy doing the paper round except when it was pouring with rain, and on many occasions I used to ask the angels to do the round for me in bad weather. Perhaps not surprisingly, they always politely refused. I often used to think that the angels could do all these wonderful miracles and yet were not willing to do my paper round for me!

It would have been the spring of 1970 when I thought about getting a full-time job as soon as I left school in order to generate more money for me to be able to spend. In those days you could leave school at the age of fifteen and even though I went to a grammar school, I thought that I would like to do exactly that: leave school in the summer of 1970 and get a full-time job in order to generate money. I really did not give much thought to a career or anything. I was more interested in just generating cash to spend from a social perspective. I'm not sure of the process for how you left school at fifteen but I recall being called into the headmaster's office on one particular day with him asking me if it was true that I wanted to leave school at fifteen.

I told the headmaster that, yes, that was indeed correct – I wanted to leave at fifteen and get a full-time job. He said to me that I would be wasting my academic career and that even though over the last year or so I levelled out in the medium group in most subjects, I was still bright enough to be able to go on and take O Levels and A Levels.

I heard everything he said but my mind was made up. I really had decided that I wanted to leave school and get a full-time job. My parents were quite supportive of me at this stage and I particularly recall my mother writing a letter to the post office asking whether or not they had any vacancies for a telegram boy. During the early 1970s, telegrams were a big thing, especially in Portsmouth, which is a naval city. I considered that to be quite a good job at the age of fifteen, going around the city delivering telegrams to various addresses.

I could sense that the headmaster and most of the teachers at Northern Grammar School were not too impressed with the idea of me leaving at the age of fifteen, and I think that they would have much preferred me to have stayed on at school to gain academic qualifications. My parents were quite supportive of the idea of me getting a full-time job, although they would have been equally happy for me to stay at school.

On one particular day, Chrystal appeared by my side while I was alone in the back garden of Orchard Road, and asked me whether I thought I was doing the right thing in leaving school. I told Chrystal that I was very keen to get a full-time job and to make my own way in life. She said that while that was commendable, there would be further opportunities for me to get a job, and perhaps an even better job later on in life should I stay at school and get the academic qualifications that the headmaster had suggested.

I told Chrystal that I really felt strongly that I wanted to get this job and unless she said anything totally to the opposite, I really would go along that route. Chrystal could tell that my mind was indeed made up. I don't think that anything that the angels said to me at that time would have changed my decision even slightly. Chrystal then said something that gave me great strength, however. She said that should I choose to get a full-time job at that point then I would still have the most wonderful of careers and all would be well for me. I was extremely encouraged by that and thanked Chrystal for saying those words. At that moment I fully decided that indeed my mind was made up. I was going to leave school and get a job.

Within a week I had received a letter back from the post office, asking me to go in for an interview for a vacancy they had for a telegram boy. I think in the letter they called it a 'young postman' position but the actual vacancy was for a telegram boy. I went in for the interview and there were two people actually conducting the interview. As soon as the door was opened for me to walk into their office, I knew immediately that I would pass, for as I was about to sit down I saw an angel behind the interviewers. I had no idea who this angel was and I had never seen her before, and have not seen her since, but I was convinced that as I had seen an angelic presence in the room that all would be well for me. Sure enough, within a week or so I received a letter confirming my appointment as a telegram boy in Portsmouth and my start date would be 24 August 1970.

I duly left school at the end of the term and went into the summer break in July 1970 knowing that I would be starting a full-time job at the end of the summer holidays. I really enjoyed my last day at school and said goodbye to all my friends with a tinge of excitement at the thought of starting work. I had no angelic presence at school on my last day so perhaps they were standing back and just allowing me to experience all of the human emotions that such a day would bring. I do remember feeling in a position of some power actually, inasmuch as here I was having my last day at school when the headmaster, the assistant head-master and most of the other teachers wanted me to stay on.

My parents would have been happy for me to stay on, just as much as they were happy for me to start work, and I felt this overwhelming surge of people that were trying to advise me in taking a different decision and to stay on at school. It was perhaps the most fundamental decision that I had made in my life but it was a decision that I had made knowing that the outcome would be good. One of the teachers had clearly felt that I was just being rebellious and said I would live to regret that day for the rest of my life. Once I had had the angelic input, I knew that he would be wrong in his comment.

I attended my first day at work on 24 August 1970 at the post office on Commercial Road in Portsmouth. I was fitted out for my telegram boy uniform and I felt incredibly excited. I had the full uniform, a cap and shoes, but the thing I liked the best was my leather pouch and a leather belt in which I would carry the telegrams when I was delivering them. Most of the boys were sixteen or seventeen and that allowed them to drive fifty-cc motorcycles to deliver the telegrams, but because I was only fifteen years of age, all of my deliveries had to be carried out on a bicycle. I remained a telegram boy for a year and they were without doubt the happiest working days of my life.

I worked quite long hours and the work was physically demanding in that I had to ride a bicycle all over the Portsmouth area delivering telegrams, but the sense of freedom that I felt while out on the road is a wonderfully happy memory for me. I made lots of great friends with the other telegram boys there at the time and I formed great relationships with four or five of the boys in particular. All of the other boys were older than me and it was while mixing with them after work that I had my first experiences of going into the pubs in the local area and drinking beer. In those days I was never once challenged about my age and that was one point where being tall certainly helped!

A couple of the telegram boys used to dress in Teddy boy clothes outside of their work time and they used to frequent a pub in an area of Portsmouth called Stamshaw. The particular pub we used to go in was called the Mother Shipton. Quite often the pub would be full of Teddy boys dressed in their outfits, as well as other boys and young men dressed in the fashions of the time. While I was not into any particular fashion and just tried to dress in a normal, fashionable way, I was quite happy to mix with all of the other groups, such as Teddy boys and so on, when we went out socially.

This was a fantastic stage of my life: I had a full-time job that I loved, I had money coming in and I had a fantastic social life with the other boys that I used to keep company with. Against today's standards, my pay would not have seemed very much, my average take-home pay being seven pounds, fifteen shillings and sixpence (which is about seven pounds, seventy-five pence in today's money). I used to give my parents two pounds ten shillings a week for keep, which left me just over five pounds a week as spending money, a luxury indeed!

I occasionally saw the trio of angels, and in particular Chrystal, during my first few months as a telegram boy, but I must admit that I was quite happy just to forge ahead with my life as it was, and felt I did not need any specific angel input in order to enjoy myself as it was. Looking back now, I'm quite horrified at even having had that thought at the time. Angels are a fantastic part of our lives, should we choose to accept them, and I would always recommend fully opening the door to angelic contact whenever that is possible. I suppose that headmaster was right; perhaps I was demonstrating a little bit of rebellion in some of my actions, and now that I was working and had some money, and now that I was enjoying a social life by going to the pub occasionally with my friends, I felt that I was receiving all I needed. While I would not say at the time that I was turning my back on the angels, I think it is fair to say I was at least halfway to turning my back on them!

At the time, when we used to go into the pubs, I used to drink exactly the same as most of the other boys did, which was a pint of brown split. This was half a pint of brown ale and half a pint of mild ale mixed together. My tolerance of alcohol grew steadily and after a few months I was quite happily able to drink up to eight pints of brown split and not have any real adverse effects. It was incredible how people's bodies are different, however, inasmuch as a couple of the boys used to be physically sick if they drank more than about three pints. My tolerance level at that time was very strong.

On one particular day during the winter of 1970, I was riding my bicycle to deliver a telegram and I suddenly became conscious of an angelic presence on my right-hand side. I could not see any angel on my right as I was cycling but I could clearly feel it. I heard the words, 'Robert, slow down, as we would like to talk to you.'

I slowed my cycling speed down and looked to my right but still could not see any angel by my side. I heard the words, however, that the angels wanted me to hear. They said that the telegram that I was about to deliver would have an extreme emotional effect on the lady I was delivering it to. Normally when I delivered a telegram, I would knock the door and wait for the person to answer and then ask if they were the name of the person on the envelope. On this particular occasion, however, the angels asked me to do that, but to actually still stand there while the lady opened the telegram. I thought this was a strange request but I was happy to do that.

As I was cycling up the last road towards the house that I was about to deliver to, I could see there was a great, bright light emanating from the front garden of the property. I knew exactly what house to stop at without even having to look at the house numbers. I stopped my bicycle and leant the pedal against the kerbstone in order to keep the bike upright and got off the bicycle. I was walking towards the front garden and the bright light that was in it, and I was suddenly aware that there were at least five angels standing close to the front door and there were other angels milling around the front garden area. They were all surrounded by this bright light. I had never seen such a sight before.

I took the telegram out of my delivery pouch and left the other telegrams that were due for delivery to different addresses in the pouch. I looked at the name on the front of the envelope, and before knocking the door, I remembered what the angel had asked me to do when I delivered the telegram. I duly knocked the door and waited for a few moments before a lady answered. I would place her as being in her mid-forties and she opened the door and gave me a nice smile and said hello.

I said to her, 'Hello, I have a telegram for you.'

For whatever reason, I did not even ask the lady whether she was the lady whose name was on the telegram; I just knew this to be the case. I gave her the telegram and she looked at the envelope and for one moment I thought she was about to close the door on me as she placed her hand on the side of the door and started to push it closed. She stopped halfway through this action, however, and opened the envelope instead. With that, the door opened fully once again as she was opening the envelope. I can only assume that the angels pushed the door back to its open position. She opened the telegram and started to read it and I was just standing on the other side of the doorstep, just watching as she was reading the telegram. In essence I was standing there purely at the request of the angels.

All of a sudden, the lady let out a gasp and stumbled forward. She just fell face forward and did not even put her hands out in front of her to break her fall. Fortunately, I was still in the same place and I held on to her and caught her as she fell to the ground. Luckily I managed to take most of her weight before she hit the ground, and I gently laid her on the path. With that, a young gentleman and a young girl came out of the house (and I would place them to be in their early twenties) and saw the lady lying on the floor. The girl let out a shriek, 'Mum!', and stood still and the boy came running over to the lady.

By this time, the lady had come to and was trying to sit up. The young man said to the lady, 'Mum, are you OK?'

I then realised that the boy and the girl in question were the lady's children. The mother said to the boy, 'It's your father,' and with that the boy picked up the telegram and started to read it.

I knew instantly that the lady's husband and the children's father had died.

The mother was crying considerably at this time, as was the daughter, with the son seeming to take up a practical stance in the position he faced. He picked the mother up, helped by myself, and proceeded to lead her back in through the front door. Neither the boy nor the girl said anything to me, although just before the front door closed the mother turned to me and she looked deep into my eyes and through her tears she said to me, 'Thank you.' And with that, the front door closed.

When I stepped back into the front garden, I was aware that, in the light around the house, all of the angels that I had seen when I rode up to the house were still there. I also noticed now that there was a man standing in the corner of the garden who had witnessed everything that had just happened. I did not need telling by anybody who he was, as it was clear that this was the husband of the lady that I had just delivered the telegram to. With that, the angels turned towards the man, one holding his hand, and the light that had surrounded them all started to fade, as did the angels and the man. The light got smaller and smaller until it became the size of a pinhead and then vanished totally.

I was really shaken up by all of this and got back on to my bike and started to ride to the next address. I have no idea how I completed the rest of my deliveries on that particular day, as the memory of what had just happened remained with me for many, many weeks. This one incident brought me back to wanting much more direct contact with the angels though.

One night I woke up in a very stark way, having had a fairly vivid dream of me delivering that particular telegram to this lady and seeing her husband standing outside after the incident once the lady had read the telegram. In the corner of the room, I saw Bella standing there. She held out her two hands towards me and started to approach the bed. She knelt down before me and placed her two hands on my shoulders and I felt the immediate comfort and support flowing through her into me. I felt great sadness for the lady I had delivered the telegram to and told Bella that I just could not get the incident out of my mind. It had also affected me socially, inasmuch as I was not so keen to go out to the pub with some of my friends. Bella gave me great comfort and support and she hugged me for at least an hour as we spoke. I asked Bella why it was that I just kept going over and over the incident in my mind and did not seem able to detach myself from it at any level.

She told me that what had happened had been a great shock to the family in question. The lady's husband had passed suddenly, without warning, of a severe heart attack. He had died within seconds of having had the heart attack. He was working abroad at the time and the telegram was sent by his employer to his wife and family as the only way of making emergency contact, as the family had no telephone.

Bella said that the reason that I felt so much emotion connected to this incident was because my sensitive nature had been totally overcome with the emotion of the situation. She said that while from a human level I felt all of the emotion that the lady had been feeling, coupled with the emotion of her two children, from a spiritual perspective the incident had taken its toll.

The next thing she told me had a significant impact on me from that moment forward. She said the main reason that I had reacted as much as I did, and was still carrying the same emotion with me, was because I had picked up the emotion of the man who had died of the heart attack. She said that once I had stood up and the front door had closed on me, I stepped back into the angel light where the man was standing in spirit form. She said, from a sensitivity basis, I had picked up all of the emotion that the man was feeling. This particular spirit had no way of speaking to his wife or his two children and his death had been sudden and had been a shocking experience to him on a spiritual level. She said everything he had had, everything he had ever loved, had been taken away from him in a second.

Bella continued by saying that the action I took on the day was commendable and I had performed in the way the angels had wanted me to. Bella said that everything that happens in life invariably has a lesson attached to it. In this particular case, the lesson for me surrounded the need to protect myself whenever I was in a position where I saw an earthbound spirit, and also to cut any ties to the situation once the contact with the spirit had finished. Bella said that she would teach me how to cut the ties to this particular incident, and to the spirit in question, so that some of the emotional feel attached to that could be transferred over to the light, which would enable me to lead my life in a more normal way. Bella asked me to lie on the bed and to close my eyes and she talked me through how to cut those ties of attachment to the situation. I did everything that Bella said and I must admit, within an hour or so, I felt much better, almost as if a great weight had been lifted from me.

Bella said that at a later date, I would be taught a lot more about protection and also have a lot more detail given to me about cutting ties and cords of attachment.

Fortunately, most of the other experiences I had as a telegram boy were of a much more uplifting nature. I particularly recall one incident when I was asked to deliver a telegram to a Royal Naval ship that was docked at Portsmouth. When I reached the base of the ship, there was a long gangplank up to the entry to the ship itself. I was particularly scared of heights (and still am) and the only way to board the ship was to go up this gangplank. The plank in question must have been at least thirty feet long and certainly did not seem very wide at all. Even though there was rope support for the handrail, I was not too keen to go up. I kept calling out to see if anyone on the ship would be willing to come down but I did not see anybody at all.

One of the mottos at the time for the telegram boys was that the 'telegram always had to get through', so I decided to pluck up my courage and start to walk up the gangplank. I got halfway up and suddenly froze. I could not take another step forward and I could not take another step back. The drop that was surrounding both sides of the gangplank had frozen me solid. With that, a couple of the sailors on-board the ship came to the top of the gangplank and saw me standing there. They asked me what I wanted. I said I was trying to deliver a telegram to somebody on the ship but I did not confess to being frozen to the spot.

One of the sailors said, 'That's fine. Bring it up here and I will take it off of you.'

I felt a right idiot, but I asked whether they would come down to collect it. At this stage I think they sensed my fear. This to them was a huge joke, but to me it was a scene of abject terror.

Both of the sailors started to laugh and said, 'Come on, bring it up here.'

I felt as though I couldn't move, but also felt ridiculed by both the sailors in question, so with that I went down on to all fours and crawled up the rest of the gangplank to give the sailors the telegram. They were laughing uncontrollably by the time I got to the top and handed the telegram to them. I did not stand up and I did not turn round; all I did was start to crawl backwards the way that I had crawled up in order to reach the safety of the bottom of the gangplank. I heard them laughing all the way down.

As I reached ground level again, I was absolutely delighted to stand up, turn around, run back to my bicycle and ride off as fast as I could, feeling absolutely ridiculed on every level. I'm not sure what the lesson was for me in this incident, but boy was I glad to get my feet back on the ground.

Throughout the remainder of my time as a telegram boy, I had many happy experiences of being at work and out on telegram delivery, and also socialising with my friends, which I had restarted following the incident with the spirit that I had encountered. The two acts of what I suppose I could call rebellion had ended up OK. The first, having left school at the age of fifteen, turned out to be fine in that I had secured a job that I loved. The second act of rebellion; half-turning my back on the angels when I started to socialise as a teenager with some of my friends, made me realise how loving and supportive the angels are. Not for one moment did the angels judge me when I turned my back on them; not for one moment would they stop supporting me; not for one moment would they cease to protect me in every way possible. Whatever we do as human beings, the angels love us unconditionally and that will always remain the case.

Family Life

Although I really enjoyed my time as a telegram boy, I was always conscious of what the angels had told me regarding my career. They had intimated that even if I had left school at fifteen, I would still forge a successful career. I was acutely aware, therefore, that I could not stay a telegram boy for ever, no matter how appealing the thought of that sounded at the time!

I was still only fifteen years of age but was conscious of the fact that the career path that would befall me would consist purely of me becoming a postman by the time I was eighteen. While it was certainly appealing to stay on as a telegram boy for three years, I must admit I was not too enamoured at the thought of becoming a postman in three years' time. With that in mind, shortly before my sixteenth birthday I applied internally within the Post Office for a promotion to the position of postal and telegraph officer. In essence, this post consisted of working within a main branch of the Post Office serving on counter duties. Should I be successful in that application, I thought to myself, then a more office-based career path would open up for me. I do not recall ever asking the angels as to whether this would be a good move for me, but I just felt intuitively that it was the right thing to do. I therefore applied for the position and was pleased once I had taken the examination, and had various interviews, to be accepted as a postal and telegraph officer.

It was with much regret that I worked my last week as a telegram boy and I remember feeling very sad at the thought of leaving the position, even though I would be based in the same premises at the post office in Commercial Road. I tried to mitigate some of the sad feelings I had at leaving the telegram-boy post with the thought of at least being able to see some of my friends that were still telegram boys, either in my lunch breaks or certainly socially in the evenings.

The training for the postal and telegraph officer position was fairly intense and I was posted to an office in Cardiff for eight weeks. The first four weeks of this posting consisted of a formal training programme at a place called Coryton House in Cardiff, to be taught all the intricacies of handling counter transactions. The second four weeks would entail me working at a branch office in Cardiff city centre (Hayes branch office) to gain experience of actually performing the various transactions that a counter clerk undertook in those days. There were a wide variety of transactions that needed to be carried out, for example pension and benefit payments, accepting telegrams for transmission, international money orders, national savings certificates, and so on.

Having come from a relatively poor family background, I had never seen so much money in all my life while undertaking the various transactions on the counter. It felt really strange, handling thousands of pounds worth of transactions on a daily basis and then, after leaving work, searching through my pockets to see if I could find the odd sixpence that I needed for bus fare to get back to my digs. I had always been taught good and strong family values from an early age and there was a clear difference between the money that I handled in a business environment and my personal money situation.

I quite enjoyed the eight weeks I spent in Cardiff, although I did feel a little homesick on occasions, spending most of the evenings alone in the room I was boarding in at the guest house arranged by the post office. The monotony and boredom that I felt some evenings was only punctuated when I had angel visitations. The most common of these would involve Chrystal appearing in my room and we would chat away for an hour or so on a wide variety of topics. I do not recall any formal training from the angels at that stage, and looking back I expect this was due to the fact that they knew that I had enough on my plate with absorbing all of the formal training that I was undertaking to carry out my role on counter duties.

At the end of the eight-week period, I returned to Portsmouth to start working on the post office counter in a full live environment. I was appointed to a branch office in a Portsmouth area called Buckland. I worked at this particular counter for quite a few months before moving on to work in many other Post Office branches in the Portsmouth area.

Between the ages of sixteen and eighteen, I enjoyed my experiences of working on the post office counter, and as well as retaining some of my friends that I had made among the telegram boys, I also made new friends with some of my colleagues on the counter. I had a very good social life at that time and enjoyed going out with my friends and doing the normal things that teenagers did at that time. I also worked very hard for the post office and used to carry out a lot of overtime duties as well as my normal standard forty-two hours a week, and was only too keen to come in and work overtime on my days off whenever there were sick absences in other post office branches. Looking back, I suppose the expression that would accurately describe those couple of years would be that I worked hard and played hard!

I had many angel visitations during that period, which to me were what I would have called at the time a normal occurrence. I also began to notice that I saw a considerable increase in the number of spirits that I would see and I would always think back to what the angels had previously told me regarding earthbound spirits. I often used to wonder how many of these spirits that I was seeing were truly earthbound, and therefore would benefit from some form of spirit rescue, and which ones were not earthbound at all but were just reappearing in spirit form for whatever reason. I particularly remember frequently seeing a spirit of a lady who was always dressed in black. She was always pushing a pram and whenever I saw her she would look intently at me, turn away and start pushing the pram while walking away from me. I always had the same emotion every time I saw this lady and that emotion would best be described as fear. I was also conscious that throughout my childhood years I used to have vivid dreams of seeing this lady in black, and even in a dream state, I always saw the same scenario of her pushing the pram away from me. I used to wake up from those dreams in a cold sweat. I began to realise that there must be something significant in the frequency that I was seeing this lady, either in real terms as a spirit, or in the visions I was having in a dream state.

On one particular day, the fear that I felt at seeing this spirit reached such a level that I promised myself I was going to talk to Chrystal about this the very next opportunity I had.

A day or so later, I was alone at home watching television when Chrystal suddenly appeared, standing between myself and the television I was watching. She literally appeared from nowhere and I had no previous inkling of her arrival, such as sensing her energy. She was just suddenly standing there.

Chrystal said that she had chosen to come to me at that time as she knew that I would be alone in the house for at least another hour or so and she wanted to talk to me about any fears I had. I instantly knew that Chrystal had picked up on my previous thoughts regarding the lady in black. Chrystal asked me why I had not called in the angels earlier to talk to about this subject or to seek their help. Chrystal said that I used to take on far too many of these thoughts alone and I needed to learn that I could call the angels at any time, either verbally, or just by thought, and they would appear should it be right to do so.

Chrystal continued by asking me to really ask myself why was it that, even though I knew all about the angels, I seemed reluctant to call them in and ask their advice. She said that all of the angels were there to help me, as indeed they are for the whole of the human race; all we need to do is ask for their help and it is their pleasure to give it, without exception. To this day I still do not fully comprehend why I do not call upon the angels more often rather than leaving it to them to instigate most of their contact with me. Both the angels and myself have now learnt to treat that issue in a rather amusing way and the angels often say to me that they know what I am like. I take that comment in an endearing way!

Anyway, getting back to the point in question regarding the lady in black, once Chrystal and I had discussed my reluctance to call the angels in on a more frequent basis, we did then move on to discuss the many sightings that I had had of the lady in black. Chrystal asked me to explain everything that I felt while seeing this particular lady in spirit form. I told Chrystal that, whether it was a physical seeing of my eyes or whether it was in a dream state, the scenario was always the same. I said that the lady would be standing there with a pram looking intently at me. Once I had made eye contact with the spirit, she would turn away from me and start pushing the pram in the opposite direction.

Chrystal acknowledged this and asked me to go further into myself and explain to her the emotions that I would feel at the time.

I said to her that what I felt was always the same: it was a fear-based emotion.

Chrystal asked me to analyse in more detail when I actually felt the fear: for example, was it when I first saw the lady? Was it when I looked into her eyes? Was it when she turned around with the pram? Or was it when she was walking away with the pram?

I thought that this was an interesting question and I must admit I found it slightly difficult to answer, but I did say that on reflection I always felt the fear at the end of the sighting. Even though the situation was always the same, I realised that I did not feel fear when I first saw the woman or when we were making eye contact. The fear was always an 'after' emotion. Chrystal said that there was no need for me to feel this fear and that I should try to engage the spirit in a way to break the cycle and to have a better understanding of who this particular spirit was.

I remember clearly saying to Chrystal that surely she knew exactly who the spirit was and asking could she not tell me. Chrystal closed that part of the conversation down very quickly and said to me that I needed to experience certain things myself and that this was one of those occasions when the angels knew that no harm would come to me but for my own development, and for the development of others, I needed to learn how to engage spirits in a more structured way.

Before leaving, Chrystal said something that was of incredible importance to me. She said that I had intimated to her that every time I saw the spirit, I always felt fear as the spirit turned and walked away from me, and I was left with the 'after' feeling of extreme fear. Chrystal said that in my mind I had interpreted that the spirit was giving me this fear, and that for some reason or another I should be afraid of her. Chrystal asked me to look at that from the other side of the fence. She asked if I had ever thought that the reason the lady turned and walked away from me was that she could sense that I was feeling this fear and she was walking away to protect me from feeling that fear any longer. She said perhaps the lady had been coming back to me so frequently, hoping that one day I would not feel the fear and that she could engage me in a conversation that was of obvious importance to her.

Little did I realise at the time that this was a major break-through for me in understanding that just because I saw this lady in spirit form and I felt fear, this did not mean that the spirit in question was creating the fear in me, and in walking away, it could literally have been the reverse: she was walking away purely because of the fear that had been created in me, and she was walking away to protect me from that. I was later to find out that this was indeed the case.

In 1974, when I was nineteen, an event occurred at Portsmouth Post Office that was to change the rest of my life for ever. Every month or so, we would have a new entrant starting on the counter that had just come back from their counter-training duties. On one particular day in 1974, a young girl of seventeen arrived to start work and she was just that one of the new entrants starting at the post office. Her name was Jackie Watson. Little did I realise at that time that Jackie was later to become my wife and the mother of my children, and within two years of meeting her we would get married and still be together some thirty-two years later.

Jackie used to have quite a bit of difficulty in balancing her counter till at the end of every week, and whereas mathematics was one of my strong points, it was not necessarily one of Jackie's strengths. I was later to find out Jackie's strengths lay in many other areas. Whether or not it was the time we spent together while I was helping her balance her till on a weekly basis, or whether or not it was just a general attraction that was growing between us, on Boxing Day of 1974 we had our first date. Jackie's mother ran a pub in Portsmouth called Cox's Hotel, which was opposite the dockyard in Portsmouth, and I must admit I found that to be of huge benefit! With me being a nineteen-year-old young man, having a seventeen-year-old girlfriend whose mother owned a pub, life just could not have been better!

I suppose, looking back against today's standards, it was a bit of a whirlwind romance because Jackie and I got engaged in 1975 and we married on 6 November 1976 at Shedfield Church, just outside of Wickham in Hampshire. The reason we married in Shedfield is that all of Jackie's family and history came from Shedfield and surrounding areas. We went on to have three children, our first daughter, called Kerry, was born in June 1978, our second daughter, Hayley, was born in April 1980 and our son Steven was born in April 1985.

By the time Steven was born, I had already been promoted from my counter and writing duties in Portsmouth Post Office to a supervisory position in Basingstoke Post Office. While I used to see the angels on a relatively frequent basis from the time I met Jackie until the time Steven was born in 1985, I never once told Jackie of these experiences. I used to see angels and spirits almost on a daily basis and many times I would have quite in-depth conversations with angels about a wide variety of topics. While Jackie probably would have been quite open and receptive to me telling her at that time of my experiences, I had tended to carry through the same self-protection routines I had had as a child, and told literally nobody of those experiences, not even my wife.

In 1985, shortly after Steven's birth, however, these spiritual experiences would take off to a whole new level. This coincided with work pressures taking off to a whole new level also. This manifested itself in me becoming what I would now call a workaholic. I used to work, work, work and spend six or seven days a week at work and left Jackie to more or less single-handedly bring up the children. I'm not proud of this but, for whatever reason, I used to work long and hard hours in order to gain further promotions and the material wealth that would bring. I felt that my absences from home would be offset by the material things that I could provide Jackie and the children; for example, bigger housing, better cars, foreign holidays, and so on.

I often wonder why I became so obsessed with work and spent most of my week at work, as opposed to enjoying more time at home with my wife and family. I think perhaps there were two main reasons for this. The first was that, as I had experienced such a poor childhood, with my parents having no money at all to give their children any luxuries in life, I always promised myself that when I had children, I would try to provide for them in such a way that they would experience so much more.

The second reason for spending so much time at work was perhaps also linked to childhood experiences, inasmuch as whatever I did at home was never good enough as far as my father was concerned. I recall such basic things like peeling potatoes at a very young age and being called 'cack-handed' and words to that effect, for not being able to do the job to the required standard. I think that example, plus many more similar such instances, created a certain perfectionism in me that made me try to achieve incredibly high standards in everything that I did at work. This drive for perfectionism in a work environment contributed significantly to the many promotions that I received. I worked my way up from telegram boy to director level, and while I hold a considerable amount of pride in that achievement, it also had its downside, with the effect that that will have had on my physical health and my enjoyment of life in general.

So, in essence, the self-generated drive for perfection that I had while at work, coupled with my desire to provide as much material wealth as I could for my family, directly resulted in me spending almost every hour possible at work.

In today's society, you hear much more about having a work–home life balance and it is obvious to me that my pendulum was stuck very firmly on the work side of that divide. I always like to think that I provided as much emotional support as was possible to my wife and children during my working life, as well as all the considerable material gains that came with my increasing salary, but with the benefit of hindsight, I really should have been much more aware myself of the work–home life balance. In later years, this would also have a considerable impact on my interactions with the angels, as my obsession with work also contributed in me once again attempting to turn my back on those beautiful beings of light.

The angels were well aware of the direction I was heading in, the way I was spending more and more time at work, and less and less time at home. I particularly remember one Sunday afternoon when Jackie was out shopping and I was at home with the children. It was a particularly sunny afternoon and the three children were playing out in the back garden. All of a sudden, a considerable light illuminated the whole of the lounge area where

I was sitting. The television turned itself off simultaneously with the appearance of this light. It was clear to me that angels had appeared in the room. After a few short moments I saw the form of two angels. Both of these were females but perhaps rather surprisingly neither of these angels were Bella or Chrystal. One was dressed in a flowing turquoise-coloured gown, whereas the other wore a yellow dress. All of the ensuing conversation was held between the angel in the turquoise gown and myself. The angel in the yellow dress said nothing at the time. I was aware of the three children still playing in the garden and could see them outside of the window and I presume the children could not see or sense anything as they continued playing, oblivious to the two angels that had suddenly arrived.

The angel in the turquoise gown said that I had been blessed with three healthy, happy children and that Jackie and I should enjoy their childhood. Angels had mentioned similar things when I was at school myself, when I had commented on many occasions of the joy and fun that children have, and the naivety and innocence that they possess. This, to the angels, was truly an endearing feature. I remember saying to the two angels that I was really pleased to see them but I asked them whether they had appeared separately from Chrystal and Bella or whether they would join us, too. Both angels smiled. I wish now that I had asked the angels their names but the conversation was flowing between us and it did not cross my mind to do that.

The angel that was doing all of the speaking said to me that they had appeared to give me some angelic advice that they felt I needed to hear. The angel said they had been well aware for many months of the excessive hours I was beginning to work at my job and also of the reducing number of hours that I was spending at home as a direct consequence of working late in the evening and weekends. While at work the angels never mentioned the term work–life balance or anything like that, but looking back now it is obvious that this is the key area they were trying to get across to me. The angels said that they were well aware that I needed to strive to reach the levels that I had set myself in my work career, and they were happy to stand aside and support that and also allow that to happen. What the angel did say, however, and this struck a bit of a chord with me, was that it was very important that I kept myself healthy in order to carry out some very important angelic work later on in life.

The angel said, 'Robert, we surround you with love and protection at all times and we try to keep you safe but human free will, and your own free will in particular, is so strong that sometimes you will pull away from the very safety and security that we are providing you.'

I was always slightly amused that the angels always referred to me as 'Robert', as all of my family and friends had always called me Bob; to this day my family and friends still call me Bob, and the angels continue to call me Robert. I asked the angels what they meant by this comment because I was certainly not aware of pulling away from them in any significant way at all. The angels said that many humans use the term 'burnout' when it comes to their work environment and they said that that would adequately reflect what could happen to me unless I was more balanced in the hours I spent at work and the intensity I put in during those hours.

I will always remember the next comment by the angel when she said to me that they carried a warning to me, a warning from the angels that I may be on a course of self-destruction, both physically and emotionally, unless I reduced the number of hours that I was spending in my work environment and the intensity of the work I was doing. The angels also said that that could cause me further emotional problems, inasmuch as it could create obsessive-type behaviours. I asked the angels what they meant by those comments. The angel said that, should I continue to put in such excessive hours and work so intensively, in later years this could manifest itself in physical problems in my stomach. She continued by saying that I was running on neat adrenaline and the human body, while needing adrenaline for the fight or flight mode, could not survive long-term adrenaline release.

I must admit at the time I felt physically well, and looking back I paid lip service to this comment. I asked her what she meant by the obsessive-behaviour comment and she said that this was a mere reflection of my inability to switch my mind off from work. I readily acknowledged this point, however, as even when I was at home with Jackie and the children, I was invariably either working from home or thinking of work, and the many challenges that I faced there. Again, however, I thought I had a handle on this and was quite happy to accept what the angels had said. I had no real intention of changing anything.

Just before the angels left, the turquoise-gowned angel made a final comment, asking me not to become so obsessed with work that I stood back from the angels themselves and spirit in general. I said to the angels that I never deliberately did this, and even in my teenage years, when I half turned my back on the angels, this was never a deliberate act: it was more a reflection of me putting my efforts and energies elsewhere.

I thanked the angels for making this point, however, and I said I loved them being in my life and I loved to be able to see them clearly and hear them clearly and hold the many conversations that we had, and I promised to never fully turn my back on them. They were so inextricably linked with me and entwined with me and the whole of my life that I could never see any situation where I would deliberately try to turn my back on them. At this point, both angels raised their hands to be in front of their bodies, about shoulder height, with their fingers and thumb pointing in the air, and I could see beams of light coming out of both pairs of hands of both the angels. These beams of light seemed to go all around my body and into my body and I felt an enormous surge of loving, warm energy. Both angels smiled and gently started to stand back, and the light gently faded away.

I felt very comforted by the visit of these angels and I did not feel in any way worried about some of the obvious warnings that were being given to me at the time. It is only now, looking back, I can see that they were giving me fantastic advice, which I was about to totally ignore. I remember then sitting down on a chair as I felt a bit strange following this particular angelic visit and I looked out into the garden and could still see the children playing, oblivious to what had just happened.

I would place the children's ages at this particular angel visit as Kerry being about nine, Hayley seven and Steven two. Kerry was always a very happy-go-lucky child; she always had a bright smile on her face and was always full of fun and liveliness. Hayley was always more of an intense child, and while she too could be very funny on occasions, she also had a deeper, more reserved nature. Steven also had a fairly reserved nature and he seemed to always receive most pleasure playing on computer games as opposed to playing outdoor, sporty-type games. I frequently saw angels all around Kerry, Hayley and Steven, as indeed I do around other children, and spoke to their guardian angels on occasions. I never once asked the three children's guardian angels what their names were and I did not at any stage ever get into deep discussions with them, as it was always clear to me that the guardian angels' primary roles were to support the child that they were with and therefore hopefully one day, when it is right, Kerry, Hayley and Steven will become much more aware of their own guardian angels. I would never force this view on anybody, even my own family. Everybody has to find their own spiritual path and proceed along that path at the pace that is right for them, whether that be in this lifetime or future lifetimes.

Some months later, I was seeing the lady in black pushing a pram on a far more frequent basis. I used to see her in my dreams and also in real life and it was always the same scenario. She always looked at me, she always turned and started to walk away, pushing the pram, and I was always left with a feeling of fear. Even though I had had in-depth discussions with the angels on this previously, it just seemed to be that the same scenario replayed itself over and over again. It was almost as if this was (as some people would now refer to it) a *Groundhog Day* situation, repeating itself over and over again. I tried to engage the lady in black and send loving thoughts and ask her if she was here for any particular reason, if she needed any form of spirit rescue, if there was any message she was trying to give me and so on, but to this day I still see this same scenario on a frequent basis and it has never changed from day one to this day.

Notwithstanding what the angels had told me regarding the potential problems of the hours I used to spend at work, I still found myself doing much the same thing. As mentioned previously, however, the material benefits of this were quite considerable. Jackie and I used to take the three children on holiday abroad every year. We went to Spain about five times, we went to the USA and we went to Australia. So from a material perspective, the children did have some wonderful holidays and hopefully some fabulous memories that they will always hold. We also moved house about five or six times and always upgraded from the preceding house to a better quality house, which coincided with my promotions at work and increases in salary. All three children did fairly well at school, with Kerry and Steven being the most academic and Hayley being the most practical.

Jackie's real passion in life surrounded animals. Jackie has a totally open heart and great empathy and compassion for all animals and all wildlife, and our home has always been a bit of an open house for any animal in need. I suppose this was also Jackie's way of using the time I was away at work effectively. She was a great mother to the three children and also a great lover of all of the animals that we had at the time and have had since.

It was not long after the visit of the two angels that I was promoted to a senior management position, still within the Post Office, to Reading, which was a divisional headquarters of the Post Office at the time. The move to Reading was to coincide with my most intense period of work, which was to last for another fifteen years or so and consist of many further promotions, to Swindon and London. Later on I will explain the challenges I faced in balancing those work pressures while trying to retain some form of spirit contact. This was a major challenge for me.

Shortly after taking up my position at the Reading office, I was working late one night when I became aware that Chrystal had suddenly joined me. I was alone in the office, preparing for an early morning presentation the next day, when Chrystal suddenly appeared in front of me. She could see that I was intently reading and preparing for the presentation that I had to carry out and she acknowledged this point by almost apologetically asking whether I would like to talk.

I leant back in the chair and thanked Chrystal for coming to see me again and said I would be pleased to talk. While looking at Chrystal, it became clear to me just how much I had become wrapped up in the presentation work that I was carrying out. Chrystal seemed to be totally translucent and the light around her was flickering. She seemed to look different to how she normally appeared. At that precise moment, I rubbed my eyes, not knowing whether the different look that Chrystal had was caused by blurred vision on my part or whether she did indeed present herself in a different format on that occasion.

Chrystal could obviously sense this because she said to me that my energy and my vibration was almost electrical at that point, and I was so immersed in my work that my whole aura and energy field was almost of static electricity. She said that while she had lowered her vibration in order to come and see me and to have this talk, my vibration was, in her words, 'all over the place'. Chrystal asked me if I appreciated what the time was and I thought I did but when I looked at the clock I suddenly saw it was 10.35 p.m., although to me it only felt about 8 p.m. I was not at all a clock-watcher at work and many nights would work close to midnight, or beyond on some occasions. I always used to arrive for work by 7 a.m. at the latest, and looking back now, no wonder the angels gave me that 'burnout' warning.

Chrystal asked me whether or not I had heeded any of the advice given to me by the two angels that had visited me previously. I was honest in my reply to Chrystal, as I always am, when I said I had indeed listened to what the angels had said but felt that I was strong enough just to carry on in the vein that I was currently in. I said that I felt fit and well, and from both a physical and emotional perspective, I was really enjoying my job and could see no downside to the hours that I was working. Chrystal smiled at this and said obviously I would need to learn lessons at my own pace. She also said that this was an example of the human free will that the angels had often told me about.

I told Chrystal that I did not deliberately intend, or even try, to go against angelic advice regarding my work hours but it was just that was how it was. I loved my job. I was committed to my job. I was totally conscientious and set myself extremely high and stretching targets. Chrystal said the angels would not talk to me again on this particular subject, but she asked me to always be aware of the advice I had been given as that advice would be true from the day it was given and would always be the case throughout my life.

Chrystal said the one point she really wanted to talk to me about, however, was the potential for me distancing myself from the angels if I became even more engrossed in work. She said that while I was not consciously aware that this may well be the case, she almost begged me to prevent that happening, and to never, ever, shut the door on the angels. I promised Chrystal this would never be the case and that I would always welcome angels into my life.

Chrystal reiterated her comment by saying, 'Robert, we are always keen to keep our contact with you open exactly as it is now and has always been, but we are equally keen to keep that contact open for the many lessons that you need to learn, and for the many teachings that you need to have in order to pass on some of our messages to the many other people that we need to hear them.'

Chrystal said this in such a calm and authoritative way that I could feel the emotion that she was expressing through her words. This obviously meant a great deal to the angels and I had no hesitation in saying to Chrystal that I would do everything in my power to always keep the door open to the angels so that I could pass on anything they wanted me to pass on, and that while I was committed and conscientious to work, and had no doubt that I would continue to work excessively long hours at a very intense pace, I would strive to ensure that this did not in any fashion stand in the way of my interface with those beautiful beings that we call angels.

Chrystal said that the angels would stand back a little over the next few years in order to allow me to concentrate on the things that I deemed important regarding work, and that while they would continue to stay in contact with me, they would not be asking me to carry out many learning opportunities.

Chrystal concluded with something that really intrigued me at the time. She said that there would come a stage in later life when I would be taking a leap of faith, a leap of faith into the world of angels. She said that the angels had told me many years previously that I would have a successful business career and that this indeed would still be the case. She said that towards the end of that business career, my vibration would be changed to such an extent that I would feel like a fish out of water in a business environment. She said that at that stage, certain doors would be open for me to receive the spiritual teachings that I needed to, in order for me to take on the next steps and to carry out some of the angel work that the angels wanted me to perform. She said that certain teachers would be presented to me, both from a human perspective and a spiritual perspective, to give me those teachings so that I could pass on the many messages and the many lessons to the other people that the angels wanted me to contact. Chrystal said that I would be taught all about the angel hierarchy, introduced to many archangels and shown some incredible sights with what we refer to as ascended masters. She said all of this would be given to me and shown to me at the right time.

I remember feeling very excited about this as well as intrigued and I asked Chrystal whether I could be shown any of those things now in order to accelerate my learning.

Looking back, how foolish of me to have asked Chrystal that; it was clear that the angels were going to stand back a bit to allow me to concentrate on my work career and that at the appropriate moment, the doors would be opened for me to be shown some truly wonderful and awesome spiritual sights. Chrystal said I could not even comprehend at that stage some of the things that I would be taught and some of the things I would be shown. She said I would be introduced to all sorts of spirits that would truly open my eyes and remove every parameter or boundary the human mind could put in the way of spiritual progression.

I remember Chrystal laughing as she looked intently in my eyes and said, and I will always remember these words until my dying day, 'Robert, what we will show you will truly blow your mind away.'

Chrystal said that with such feeling, it was impossible not to feel a tingle of excitement and anticipation at what I was to be shown at a later date. The thought that I had been chosen to also pass on those angelic teachings, some of which will be in this book, also made me feel very humble.

Chrystal then smiled and said that she would leave me to work on my presentation and to always remember that she and all of the other angels were just a thought away. On this occasion,

Chrystal instantaneously vanished as opposed to fading away. I must admit, Chrystal gave me so much to think of with what she had said that I found it impossible to concentrate on the presentation, so within a matter of five minutes or so I had decided to lock all of my files and folders away in my desk drawer and go home and have something to eat and drink, hopefully have a good sleep, with the firm intention of arriving for work about 6 a.m. the next day in order to finish off the presentation, ready to carry it out later that morning.

Little did I realise at that time the magnitude of what Chrystal had told me. The spiritual experiences that the angels were to give me later in life were indeed truly awesome. If anything, Chrystal understated what the angels were going to show me and teach me. I consider it my greatest honour in life to have been taught by God's own messengers, the angels.

Balancing Work and Spirit

Even after my latest encounters that I had had with the angels, and in particular Chrystal giving me the subtle warnings about balancing my work life and my personal life, I tended to ignore that advice and I continued to throw myself into my work. I actually worked for Royal Mail for a period of thirty-two years and one week, between 24 August 1970 and 31 August 2002. I was totally dedicated, conscientious and always strived to achieve a quality output in all that I did. I was very customer focused in all of my work and I also consider myself to have been an excellent team player.

In 1997, I was promoted to director level within Royal Mail and this was indeed a very senior position. Being such a high achiever, I put tremendous pressure on myself to deliver high quality standards in all of my work. Looking back now, I could perhaps have delivered my work to about seventy per cent of the level that I did and I am sure that my employers would have still been delighted with the output that I achieved. I maintained a drive for perfectionism, however, in everything that I did and this contributed to me putting one hundred per cent effort into everything. Throughout the last five years of my working career, I was working on a six- to seven-day-week basis continuously, with most days starting very early in the morning and finishing very late in the evening. I was never asked to work these excessively long hours by my employer – far from it. I worked for excellent managers within the Royal Mail, who had commented on many occasions that I needed to strike a better balance between my work and home life (just as Chrystal and the angels had always told me), but my drive for perfectionism was so intense I ignored all of the advice given and continued to work at breakneck pace.

While I placed those standards on myself and worked the excessive hours in order to deliver the many outputs that I set myself, I am pleased to say that I considered myself to be an excellent leader throughout my time in Royal Mail, and I always made sure that those who worked for me had a much better balance between their work and personal lives. It was perhaps much easier for me to encourage others to have that balance, whereas when it came to myself, I found that an impossibility.

Throughout those last five years, perhaps not surprisingly when one considers the intense pace that I was working at, the angels tended to stand back much more than they had done previously and my contact with them was far more infrequent. While I used to regularly see spirits and angels throughout those last five years of my Royal Mail career, I tended not to engage in dialogue with them unless I was specifically asked to do so. I am not proud to say this, but looking back, there must have been many spirits that I could have helped but didn't. Certainly in terms of spirit rescue, but by not engaging in dialogue with them, I missed the opportunity to assist them in whatever way would have been appropriate.

Between the years 1997 and 2000, I was based in Swindon and used to travel to and from my home in the Portsmouth area to the Royal Mail's Swindon office, which was a journey of about one and a half hours each way. I used to leave home at approximately 5 a.m. daily and most days would not arrive back home until about 10.30 p.m. This allowed very little time to actively engage in spirit dialogue. While I continued to see the trio of angels throughout this period, both Amhiel and Chrystal were a lot more distant than had hitherto been the case. I perhaps saw much more of Bella, who regularly used to visit me at night, which I am sure was more of Bella giving me a comforting gesture rather than her engaging me in any form of serious dialogue. To this day, I really appreciate her doing that.

In the year 2000, I was appointed to another senior director position within Royal Mail, but this time I was based in London. To offset some of the considerable travelling that I was doing, Royal Mail provided me with a flat at the Barbican Centre. I more or less lived at the flat for the next two years and only travelled home late on a Saturday just to spend the Saturday night at home and then used to go back up to London on Sunday evening, ready for the beginning of the working week. Looking back, Jackie was so incredibly supportive of my working career and the incessant demands that I placed on her by working such long hours. She really was a jewel in the crown for supporting me throughout my working career. There is a saying, 'Behind every successful man there is a good woman.' Well, in my case, while I can certainly say, yes indeed, I was very successful, I was fortunate enough to have a great woman by my side. None of what I have achieved would have been possible without the fabulous support that Jackie gave me.

Even though most of the time I was working away, I always still tried to contribute in whatever way I could in terms of being a father figure to the children and to be a supporter of the family. I think I achieved that quite well because to this day Jackie and I are blessed with our three children still keeping in close touch with us, even though they now live in their own homes and have their own lives. I think it is fair to say that the children see me clearly as the head of the family and they know that every contribution that I give them comes directly from my heart and I always try to advise them appropriately if they ever come to me for advice.

From about 2001 onwards, I really began to feel a shift in my attitudes to my work and my distancing myself from the angels. I knew something of significant magnitude was about to happen to redress the balance, but little did I know just how significant this shift would be.

Searching for Truth

On one beautiful day during the summer of 2001, I was standing in my apartment in London looking out of the patio window at the skyline of the surrounding area. It was a Saturday afternoon and I had been previously working on the lounge table and there were many papers spread around it. I had stood up just to clear my head and to have a little stretch. I suddenly saw this incredibly bright light, which seemed to be just the other side of the patio window. It appeared to me at the time that there must have been a giant searchlight that had been shone in the direction of my flat. I know now that may have been a silly assumption but I really could not explain the brightness of the light and how it just appeared to be on the other side of the patio glass. I could certainly see that it was not a reflection of the sun but at the time I could not explain what I was seeing. I will try to give an explanation here that will help the reader visualise exactly what I was seeing.

Just the other side of the patio glass, there was a bright light that was shining into the lounge area of my flat. It totally engulfed me and most of the lounge that was behind me. I would place the light at being about three feet in diameter and it was circular in appearance. The light itself was oscillating, and while it was an incredibly bright, white light, I could clearly see movement within it. This circular, vibrating light was almost pulsing like a heartbeat. I was totally intrigued by this and I felt no fear whatsoever; suffice it to say my feelings were much more of excitement and intrigue.

I suddenly heard a voice behind me and turned round to see the most majestic of all angels. The angel was of male presence but was dressed in white robes and had brilliant white hair. I could not see any angel wings whatsoever but I certainly could sense that this being was of a similar vibration to those from the angelic realms. The gentleman held out his two arms in a beckoning sort of movement and smiled. He had a full white beard, and what with his white hair and white robes, he certainly looked a majestic sight. Knowing what I know now, this being was not an angel as we see them today, but he was from a dimension where he had similar attributes to those from the angelic realms.

He emitted pure love. This is perhaps hard to describe in simple words; in fact, it would be better to say this is impossible to describe in words. The sheer immense pleasure that one receives from standing in the exalted company of somebody from the realms of pure love is impossible to describe. It is a heartfelt connection that is instantaneously made and a connection where no words are needed. I was very fortunate, however, for this being to talk to me and to give me an insight into some of the wonderful things that would shortly befall me. I am not sure how long I stood there looking at this gentleman before he spoke; it may have been just a minute or two, but equally it may have been an hour or two.

He spoke in a very soft, calm manner and I am not sure whether he just chose his words carefully or whether, and this is more likely, all of his words were direct from a love source and therefore would always be words of great magnitude. He introduced himself not by name but by saying he had come from a realm where pure love existed and that he wanted to share something with me that I would need in future years. I was hanging on his every word.

I do recall, however, at some stage, asking him what this bright light was, which by that stage was behind me as I was now facing into the lounge. He smiled and said that the simplest explanation that I would understand would be that it was equivalent to a portal between our earthly world and the spirit world.

He asked me to not analyse the current situation but just to accept it as it was. He smiled, however, and said that at some stage in the future many of the questions that I had would be fully answered. I took some comfort in this, knowing that my analytical business mind often wanted answers to many things that I saw spiritually. I later learned that many of the things that exist in the spirit world, and indeed between our two worlds, just cannot be explained for human comprehension. While the human brain is a fantastically powerful equivalent of a human computer, it just cannot comprehend many of the things that exist in the world of spirit.

The gentleman continued by saying to me that he had taken the opportunity to come to me at this particular moment because the time was right for me to start to unravel some of the things that I needed to put in place to make the significant contribution that they required of me in later life. He could sense all of my thoughts almost before I thought them, and so I really did not need to speak much in answer to his points. In fact, anything I did say was of a rather tongue-tied nature and I feel that this was because I was well aware that I was in the presence of somebody great. In later chapters, I will explain in a little more detail about this gentleman, and some others like him that I have affection-ately called the 'white people'.

He continued by saying that I had achieved much in my working career, and indeed, considering the childhood I had experienced, I had achieved considerably more than one could have thought possible. He mentioned something along the lines of human beings being like a mosaic of all of their experiences and, for me, my childhood will have contributed directly to the outlook that I took at work. He quoted an example of this: my drive for perfection was based on the fact that as a child I felt I could do no right, and this directly resulted in my perfectionist stance throughout my working career. While one could look upon this as perhaps a negative consequence, I think the point he was trying to get across was that, even though I had to face extreme adversity throughout much of my childhood, this had manifested itself in a positive way in much of what I had achieved at work. I think it is fair to say that while he was not condoning the hours or intensity that I applied to work, he was just showing how my childhood adversity reaped rewards later in my drive for a more perfect output at work. In essence, it was my working career that provided the material benefits that my family and I had enjoyed throughout my working life.

While these benefits may not have been excessive in any way, I do consider myself fortunate to have enjoyed the comforts of relatively nice houses and some excellent family holidays, for which I will always be truly grateful. The gentleman did not dwell much on what I had achieved, however; he was far more interested in saying that I was shortly to reach the crossroads of my working career and that certain decisions would need to be taken.

At the time, I thought he was referring to potential new job offers or something of that ilk, little realising that this was a precursor to some major, fundamental changes that I would need to make in order to continue on my spiritual journey. He smiled throughout his time with me and I was particularly happy when he spoke about Amhiel, Bella and Chrystal. At no stage did he mention their names but I knew that he was referring to them when he said that those who walked closest with me had taken a step back to allow me to concentrate on the matters that I considered to be important. I will always remember this because I was clearly under the impression that this gentleman was alluding to the very fact that the matters that I deemed to be important were not important at all. I did not question him on this but that was a prevailing thought that I had while he was talking to me. He obviously picked this up from me instantaneously because he said at one stage that he was not criticising the actions that I had taken, and the actions that indeed I would be taking, but what he did say, and he said this very eloquently and very clearly, was that my priorities would be changing in the very near future.

I did not ask any questions regarding this comment and just accepted it at face value. He then asked me to sit down, as he wanted to ask me some questions. I did not feel that this was odd in any way, as many of my discussions with Chrystal and Bella had taken place while I was sitting down, and having what one would describe as an everyday chat with them.

He asked me whether I had carried out any meditation in the last year or so. I knew that the answer to this was no, as indeed he did. He reminded me that meditation is an excellent way for us to still our busy minds, which then provide a platform for a more direct and better-balanced spiritual connection. He said I was very fortunate in being able to see spirits and angels as clearly as I did, whatever the state of my busy mind. I did not realise at the time just how right he was in this comment and it is only later in life that I have found out that the vast majority of people are just not blessed with the ability to see spirits as clearly as I can, even without the need for any meditation work.

The gentleman continued by asking me to say what I felt was important at that time of my life. I perhaps rather stage-managed the reply by going through the normal checklists that anyone probably would give. I said to him my wife, children, family, work, pets, and so on, were all important to me. He smiled at this and said something that I thought was a little strange at the time, but I obviously now know better. He continued by saying that anything that I truly loved deeply within my heart is the top of any priority list. By saying that, I think he was clearly inferring to me that my wife, children, pets and family and suchlike could certainly be at the top of my priority list, but that work per se, and any other material factors, were not necessarily of anywhere near the same importance. While he readily accepted that there is a balance needed for work in order to generate what we perceive to be important in terms of material wealth, we needed to be always mindful of the need to ensure our priorities were only based on a love vibration and that that should therefore drive our actions.

I presumed at the time that he was going to take me into the similar areas that Chrystal had taken me in regard to having a better balance between my work and home lives. While that may well have been a minor point of some of the things he was saying, by far the greater point that the gentleman was trying to get across to me, however, was the need for me to shortly re-establish my priorities so that I could understand exactly what was meant by the term 'love vibration' and have a far greater understanding of perhaps where this gentleman himself came from.

He asked me to close my mind totally and at the same time as doing this, he raised his right hand and placed his palm quite close to my forehead. I instantaneously felt an energy source flow between us and almost felt as though I was drifting off into a deep meditative state. He asked me a similar question again regarding my priorities, but this time I was not thinking in my mind of the answers to give him. I could hear his words, and perhaps more importantly, feel his words, direct in my heart. This, again, is an impossible thing for me to try to explain but it was almost as though he was talking directly to my heart, with my mind having no input to the dialogue whatsoever. In fact, from that moment on, I did not speak again directly by voice. The gentleman picked up everything he needed to know by the feelings and emotions that I expressed in response to any question he asked.

I cannot recall all of the individual questions but I could summarise them as being generally based on what was important to me, what gave me enjoyment, what love I felt for other people and what love I experienced in terms of world catastrophes. This was perhaps the strangest dialogue that I had ever encountered but I think it stood me in good stead to understand in far greater detail the difference between a human mind and a human heart's feeling. The lesson that I learnt during this exchange was to be of great use when I better understood the different ways that we can communicate with spirits and angels. I already had some experience of these in terms of seeing, hearing, feeling and thought.

I am not sure how long this exchange went on for but I felt totally relaxed throughout the time that the white gentleman was with me and I'm not sure how the session eventually finished other than having a clear recollection of him smiling at me and walking towards the white light that was still outside my patio window. I did not see him go into the white light at all, but needless to say both he and the light itself vanished very quickly. I was not sure at the time whether I was to receive anything from having had the session other than the feeling of total calmness and love that had befallen me, and at the time I interpreted the exchange as a spirit wanting to know how I was feeling on a wide variety of topics.

It was probably from that moment on that I knew some of the changes that Chrystal had inferred, and that this gentleman had clearly forecast, would shortly take place. Perhaps it is also right to say that I also felt differently regarding work. While I was still committed to the job, totally conscientious and loyal, in my heart things just felt different. From that moment on, it was never to be the same.

Throughout the remainder of 2001 and the first six months of 2002, I began to develop what I could best describe as a deep-down unhappiness with my work situation. I was feeling a deep longing for something, but I was not sure what. I was beginning to feel like a fish out of water in boardroom discussions with other senior colleagues. Whereas previously I had always considered it easy to contribute to boardroom discussions and senior director discussions, I began to feel that the environment was totally alien to me. I was still striving to be a perfectionist in everything that I did, however, and I would describe this as trying to overachieve in every way possible in my mind, but I was feeling the manifestation of this in my stomach. I feel that the physical effects of my work life were directly manifesting itself in my body running on neat adrenaline; this is probably why I experienced stomach problems at the time.

I could clearly feel my sensitivity rising. I was always a sensitive child, and this persisted throughout my adult life, but I could feel that this sensitivity was increasing exponentially. I was seeing angels on a far more frequent basis, and while I was seeing my trio of angels regularly, I was also seeing other angels, either in clusters or as individuals, as a regular occurrence. I am pleased to say that it was during this time that I really began to open back up to the angelic realms and I was pleased to re-engage the angels in conversations.

Little did I realise at that time that an accident I had had at the back end of the year 2000 was a signal from the angels for me to slow down. I remember on many occasions that the angels had commented to me that I was on the point of approaching a crossroads in my life. I had also been seeing, clairvoyantly, traffic light symbols, with most of the traffic lights being stuck on red. This was clearly a spiritual warning to me that I was not heeding whatsoever. The deep longing that I was experiencing, which also manifested itself in my deep unhappiness in my work environment, has since been explained to me as 'my calling' coming to the fore. The angels had tried everything possible to engage me in conversation throughout the last few years and rather recklessly I just put my head down and carried on doing things in exactly the same way that I always had.

After the visit from the white gentleman, this was clearly going to be the time when I had to listen to what spirit was saying to me.

Stopped in my Tracks

As I have previously mentioned, I had an accident on 30 December 2000 that resulted in me fracturing three vertebrae in my thoracic spine. I was hospitalised for some considerable time thereafter. I was placed in a full body brace for six months once I had left the hospital and this obviously prevented me from working to anywhere near the level that I had.

For many weeks I was on extremely strong tablets and was off sick from work. Needless to say the angels saw me, and I'm sure they will not mind me saying it in this way, as a sitting target, and the angel visits were very frequent during this time. I think the reason for this was twofold: firstly, to provide me with comfort and support during a very stressful period for me in being laid low, and secondly, to develop the readiness within me to take the next spiritual steps that the angels wanted.

I did not realise that this accident would have such a severe bearing on me when I returned to work. I actually returned to work in June 2001 and went back firing on all cylinders, almost as if I had not been away. My intensity and perfectionism was as strong as ever and I continued to achieve for Royal Mail in every way possible. As mentioned previously, my return coincided with my appointment to London, where I continued on the fast pace that I had always set regarding my work.

I obviously went back to work far too early, in any event, because I was experiencing quite considerable spinal pain and still had fairly severe spinal nerve damage. While the three vertebrae in the spine had more or less healed, the actual muscle and nerve damage that the fractures had caused were manifesting themselves in terrific pain and immobility. I had severe problems across both shoulder blades, throughout all of the thoracic spine and my neck. I tried to disguise this from work as far as possible and always gave the impression that, while I did have some problems, this in no way affected me in my work output.

From the time I had my accident in December 2000, I hid from Royal Mail the severity of the injury and the effect that it had on me and even though Royal Mail knew that I had the spinal fractures and was a fantastic employer in providing me with everything possible, I never once admitted to the sheer agony that I experienced having returned to work. Each day was like torture: the pain in my spine and the nerves associated with it was intense, but even that was not enough to stop me in my drive for achieving high-quality output. Looking back now, I clearly see this accident as being the opportunity when I really should have re-evaluated my life and decided what I wanted to make of it from that moment on. I failed to do this, however, and just continued on exactly the same path that I had been on for the thirty-odd years prior to it.

It became increasingly clear to me that I was not in any physical shape whatsoever to continue to achieve the outputs that I had set myself. From early 2002 onwards, I felt as though I was swimming against the tide. I was desperately keen to deliver the same output that I had previously delivered throughout my Royal Mail career but it was becoming increasingly difficult for me to sit at the desk to do my daily work, to sit in chairs, to attend meetings and even to stand up and give the presentations that I used to love doing.

I hid all of this from everybody within Royal Mail, other than my secretary at the time, a lady called Liz Lambourne, and it is fair to say that she was my rock for the last ten years of my working career within Royal Mail. She was a fantastic and fabulous secretary on every level. Her work was superb and she was always willing to go the extra mile in order to meet my insatiable demand for quality output. I could not possibly mention my Royal Mail career without thanking Liz for all that she did for me throughout those last ten years. No director could ever ask for a more loyal and conscientious secretary, and my debt to her is immeasurable.

In mid-2002, it became increasingly clear to me that I could not continue with my career. The pain that I was experiencing and the difficulty I had with regard to mobility made it impossible for me to continue. I spoke to senior colleagues within Royal Mail and also the Royal Mail medical team, as well as the health care consultants that I had been having contact with since my original accident, and it became clear to me that taking early retirement was the only option available to me.

Royal Mail was a fantastic employer to me throughout those thirty-two years and one week of my career, and I like to think that I returned the faith that they had in me by a factor of tenfold with my dedication and the output that I achieved for them. It was with great sadness that I took early retirement from the business on 31 August 2002.

For many weeks thereafter, the most surprising thing happened. I saw no angels and no spirits for weeks. It was almost as though I had been cast aside. No matter how much I tried, I could not see any angels and by not seeing them, I felt I could not talk to them. I felt great sadness and frustration at having had to leave work early, and here, in my moment of need, I felt as though the angels had deserted me. Following on from the visit I had from that white gentleman, I felt that once I had left my work the angels would be there in abundance, telling me what they wanted me to do for the next steps. How wrong I was. I felt alone, I felt depressed, I felt tremendously run down and I also felt that I had no purpose in life.

This must have been a truly awful period for Jackie, as I know just how low I got during this time. I was still physically suffering considerably as a result of my spinal damage but this was magnified immensely by what I considered at the time as a total desertion of me from the angels. This feeling went on for months and months. Most nights, and during the day on some days, I begged the angels to come back to me. I begged Amhiel, Bella and Chrystal to visit me, to talk to me, to explain the position that I was now in, but nothing was returned. I had forgotten anything I had previously been taught by the angels and just went into myself, deeper and deeper.

Many months passed and perhaps I now have a better understanding of just how dire the situation can be for people who suffer from depression.

While I did not in any way have a physical or chemical form of depression, I certainly felt depressed as a result of the situation that I found myself in. I felt tired, lethargic and listless. To go from everything that I had, and indeed everything that I was, to what I had now become was a terrible wrench and a terrible situation for me.

Notwithstanding this, after a period of a year or so, I began to feel as though I needed to make a change from the way that I was. It was a totally untenable situation for Jackie at the time and I commend her for hanging on in there. I was still not seeing any angels or spirits but I began to feel myself that I needed to make a change from the present spiral of depression and gloom that I was currently in. I began to go out for the odd walk. I lived quite near some wooded areas and I used to get encouragement from walking among nature. I began to feel myself feeling brighter. I still terribly missed the angels, however, and in particular Amhiel, Bella and Chrystal, and for the first time in my life I felt alone and separated from the angels and spirits generally. I suppose, looking back, throughout most of my working career I had tended to turn my back on the angels, and rather perversely I was feeling that the angels were now turning their back on me. How wrong I was. Angels never, ever turn their back on us; they love us unconditionally.

The reason that I was not seeing them and hearing them during my period of 'living in the dark' was a direct result of me. I did not realise this at the time and blamed the angels as the easy opt-out, asking them why they had turned their back on me. In fact, the opposite was true. I had immersed myself in such a deep trench that my whole vibration had changed. While I was asking for the angels to appear, I was doing all of this with my 'head-mind'; at no stage did I really open my heart to them. Perhaps I did not really even want them to appear; I just wanted to wallow in the doom and gloom that I had created for myself. If only I had really opened my heart during this period and had really felt the emotions and displayed the emotions that I was inwardly feeling, then the angels would have been there like a shot. I had created an environment where I was self-blocking them. Whereas I felt terrible at the time, with hindsight, they must have felt ten times worse, seeing me struggle, seeing me so depressed and trying so hard to contact me, but with me, without knowing this at the time, blocking them out.

By this time, and it must have been late in 2003, I began to feel my spiritual calling once again, yearning deep within me. I felt an insatiable need to start to research spiritual development and courses of that ilk on the internet. It was during one such moment when I was sitting there on the computer, looking for spiritual development courses, that I suddenly became aware of the presence of Amhiel, Bella and Chrystal all around me. I turned around on the chair that I was sitting on and saw them. All three were looking deeply into my eyes and I could feel the sheer sense of love and emotion flowing from them. I stood up immediately and threw my arms out to the three of them. They all stepped forward and the four of us were there hugging. I'm never sure how it works when an earthly person is hugging a spirit form, and in real terms of course you do not feel the same physical contact, but their energy is such that you feel this incredible warmth, this incredible love, radiating through every fibre of your being.

I had never seen or witnessed angels expressing any form of tearful emotion, but if the angels could have cried during that moment, then they surely would have. The emotion and love that I felt for them and from them was absolutely incredible. There are, again, no words that could describe this; the euphoria of being reunited with my trio of angels was the most magnificent experience that I had ever encountered. I was blurting out words at a hundred miles an hour. I was saying things like, 'Where have you been? I have been in a terrible place! I have called you, I have spoken to you – why did you not answer me?' and I continued to blurt out such utterings for the next few minutes.

Bella was the first one to speak and comforted me greatly with the words, 'Robert, we have never been away from you; we have always been here. You have shut us out. It is our greatest joy that you have once again opened yourself to receive the love that we have for you.'

Words cannot describe the sheer joy that I felt at hearing those few words from Bella and feeling the emotions of the three. From that moment on, I pledged to never again block the angels out of my life. They leave a void that is impossible to fill and never again will I allow myself to block them out.

At this stage Amhiel started to take a few steps back before totally disappearing, followed fairly quickly by Bella. I held my hand out, trying to hold Bella's hand as she moved further away from me, but she was giving me a comforting look, a look that I knew meant that she would be returning imminently. I was pleased to see this. Chrystal and I then went into my lounge and we both sat down and talked for a considerable time about the experiences that I had had over the preceding year or so.

Chrystal listened intently to everything that I had to say but kept reminding me throughout the discussion to learn to talk directly from my heart and not my head. She said that my head-mind had achieved considerable results throughout my working career, but as a child needs to learn to walk slowly and carefully, I needed to learn to communicate direct from my heart. This was a challenge I readily would accept.

Chrystal said that she was really pleased that I could feel the calling within me, which was now getting stronger by the day. She said to me that she would be prompting me on a whole range of issues but one of these would be that at some stage I would be called upon to teach others all that I had been taught. I readily agreed to do this. She also said that I would be called upon to heal others. Again, I readily agreed to do this in whatever form that took. She said I also needed to learn to speak my truth, and that truth would come directly from my heart. I readily accepted that what I previously thought was the best in my working life would not necessarily be the best for what I needed to do in terms of developing further on the spiritual path. I fully accepted that I needed to understand the difference between my head-mind thoughts and those that come from my heart and come from the position of love.

Chrystal said that only love is real. When she said this, I could see that she was bringing out some of the things that the white gentleman had mentioned to me a couple of years earlier. I'm not sure how long Chrystal and I were in conversation but I continued to talk at one hundred miles an hour. Chrystal then said to me that she would now go and leave me alone for a while so that I could just absorb our reunion and the emotions that that had created. She said that she would be holding many talks with me over the weeks and months ahead to help me make the right choices on my spiritual path, for after all it was the angels that wanted me to teach all that I know and therefore it was only right for me to listen to them to ensure that I received the best possible teachings.

Chrystal started to stand up and gave me a loving look as she suddenly started to disappear. I was left with a feeling of immense love and pride. From that moment on, I committed to myself to creating a much stronger link with the angels than I had previously and this time also committed to myself that I would listen intently to what they had to say. I know all about human free will and I know all about humans believing that we know what is best but now that I had the clear opportunity to listen to input direct from the angelic realms, steering the next steps that I intended to take, I would have been a fool not to follow that advice.

What followed was the advice I needed in order to make further progress along my spiritual path, a path that would consist of many fantastic and wonderful teachings but would also be interspersed with teachings that were not from a good source. This enabled me to readily begin to identify what were highest good teachings and what were not. I learnt many lessons throughout my formal spiritual development years and one of the major lessons concerned the need for all those on the spiritual path to be very discerning as to where they go for their teachings.

I will cover much more of this in detail later within this book.

A Spiritual Path

Having taken the sad decision to leave work but also having determined to reconnect with the angels, I decided to explore the various options open to me in terms of following a spiritual path. For many years I had been in a business environment and this was now my opportunity to become the true me. I committed myself to exploring a whole range of spiritual teachings and to see where they took me. At this early stage of my spiritual development, I really did not know where the path would lead. All I did know, and I knew this with great clarity, was that the time was now right for me. I was drawn to anything that had the word 'psychic' or 'spiritual' in its title. I looked at a whole range of websites on the internet, I attended the odd one or two psychic and spiritual fayres and I went into new-age shops, such as crystal shops, and picked up literally hundreds of leaflets advertising all manner of spiritual teachings.

Being faced with such a wide variety of topics, I really was at a bit of a loss as to what particular course or event to attend. I was a little bamboozled by the vast array that I could select from. I really did not appreciate in those early days just how vast spiritual teachings were and the amount of people that had an interest in these subjects. I remember one particular day when I was sitting on the settee, thumbing through many leaflets and reading all sorts of articles in some books that I had purchased. I was suddenly aware of a presence standing in front of me and looked up to see Chrystal looking down upon me and smiling.

She was standing about five feet away from me, dressed in a long, flowing golden robe. On this particular occasion, she had her two hands next to each other, with the palms facing upwards and she was holding a book. She was smiling at me in what I can best describe as a knowing way. She obviously could see and feel that I was rather confused by the amount of options that were open to me and that perhaps I needed a little bit of guidance. I was delighted to be able to lean back in the settee and say to Chrystal how surprised I was by the amount of literature there was concerning spiritual teachings.

Chrystal smiled and nodded in agreement. I asked her what particular course she felt I should go on. Again, Chrystal smiled at that and said that I had not learnt many lessons! She reminded me that the angels were not here to run our lives for us; they were here to guide us and support us, but not to actually make decisions for us. She asked me to slow down, and she told me that a spiritual path is a never-ending journey. You never arrive at your destination, all you can do is follow the path and be open and receptive to the many lessons and teachings that will be on your particular path.

Chrystal continued by advising me that many of my business traits and the vast business acumen that I had obtained over the preceding years were obviously of great strength in certain circumstances, but equally, these many strengths could actually be a hindrance to the work I now needed to do in following my particular spiritual path. She said that one of the most obvious issues that I would need to address, relatively early on, would be my aptitude for immediately thinking everything through with my head-mind as opposed to feeling and allowing my heart to contribute to my decision-making process.

Chrystal did not give me any specific advice on this occasion but one thing she did say certainly helped me enormously. She said that I had been truly blessed in having such a strong angel contact, which had been with me from birth, throughout my life. She also said that, in my particular instance, this contact was totally natural and unforced and in essence I did not have to make any effort at all in order to be able to see and hear angels with great clarity. But what Chrystal did say, however, was that there were a wide variety of lessons to be learnt on a spiritual path and she suggested that I learn these lessons in the same way that a baby learns to walk.

I was a little surprised by this and asked Chrystal what she meant by that comment.

Chrystal continued by saying that a baby learns to walk over many weeks and many months; it does not expect and could not possibly achieve the ability to walk overnight.

I laughed at that and said something similar in that I strongly picked up the message that I needed to walk before I could run, in terms of true spirituality.

Chrystal again nodded and smiled at that, knowing that I had clearly picked up the point that she was trying to get across. I asked Chrystal why she was holding the book and whether the book itself had any relevance to me. She said that this book was a gift from spirit to me, a gift from the angels themselves, to aid my knowledge and aid my learning. She asked me to close my eyes and to breathe slowly and deeply. I started to do this but was immediately taken aback, feeling that I needed to take a sharp intake of breath. I felt as though my whole body went rigid and I was almost short of breath. I suppose I can best describe this feeling as the feeling that you have as a child if you run into somebody or something and get winded, the feeling that you cannot breathe, the slight feeling of fear that you begin to feel at that very moment. Well, this is exactly the same feeling that I had now with Chrystal.

I remember still having my eyes closed but being rather short of breath and all of a sudden it was as though I had received a minor electric shock, as my body tingled from head to toe. At that stage I looked up and Chrystal was still standing in front of me, but this time a little closer to me, smiling and holding her hands out with the palms facing towards me.

The book had vanished and I remember saying to Chrystal, 'Wow, what was that?'

Chrystal laughed at that and said I had been given a gift by the angels, a beautiful gift bestowed upon me from the angels, and even now my analytical mind tried to analyse this rather than just accepting it lovingly and unconditionally, in the manner that the angels intended.

I too smiled at this, noting the comments that Chrystal had made.

Chrystal said no more on this particular subject and just smiled and started to take a couple of steps back before vanishing from the room altogether. I recall sitting on the settee for a few moments, still trying to analyse what had just happened to me.

Whether this is right or wrong, I just assumed that the angels had given me the gift of some form of knowledge that I might need at some stage to help me, and hopefully many others, on the spiritual path and their own relevant spiritual journeys.

It would have been so much simpler if I had learned the lesson there and then not to engage my head-mind, my business mind, in my dealings with the angels but for many years thereafter I still fell into the trap of trying to analyse things that were beyond human comprehension.

After composing myself, I decided to go and make a cup of tea and to come back and collect all of the leaflets up and put them in a bag until I was ready to review them again. Just before I walked out into the kitchen, however, one particular leaflet caught my eye. This leaflet advertised a chakra meditation course. The leaflet seemed to be much bolder than the others and it just caught my eye and certainly stuck out against the many leaflets that were by now lying around the floor.

I picked this particular leaflet up and immediately felt drawn to the content of the course. It spoke about chakras, a word I had heard of but had not specifically understood. It said that the course would be for a twelve-week period and would cover the chakras in a human body and also would encourage each of the attendees to be trained (if I can call it that) in meditation tech-niques. As I said, this particular course did appeal to me and I certainly saw it as a course that would be in sync with the points that Chrystal made to me regarding the need to learn to walk rather than run. The course did say that it was aimed at beginners and I thought that this indeed would be a good opening for me in following some form of spiritual path. I immediately telephoned the organiser of the course. I was lucky enough to be able to book myself a place and was also delighted when I spoke to Jackie about this and she agreed that it would be useful for her to attend the course as well.

A couple of weeks passed before the course actually started and most of the time between my booking the course and the course actually starting was taken up with further research on the internet and reading all sorts of literature on spirit matters. I completed the whole of the twelve weeks of the meditation course, feeling that it would give me a good baseline for more advanced courses at a later date. Jackie, however, left after a couple of weeks to attend specific animal-healing courses at another venue. Animal welfare is indeed Jackie's soul destiny.

I learnt many things on the chakra meditation course and some of the basics of these concerned the seven main chakras that are contained within the human body.

There is the root chakra at the base of the spine; the sacral chakra, which is in the lower stomach area; the solar plexus, which is in the middle stomach; the heart chakra; the throat chakra; the brow chakra and the crown chakra. This part of the book is in no way meant as a teaching guide to the chakras but anybody interested in following a spiritual path could do worse than learning about the chakras within the human body and the benefits of understanding these and their main purpose.

As well as learning about the chakras, it was also very useful to have a thirty-minute meditation at the end of each lesson. This definitely gave me experience of meditating in a group environment and I found that to be of some use, as the energy of the room would change considerably if there were many people meditating at the same time. While I had very rarely carried out any form of singular meditation prior to this course, I could sense and feel the benefits of doing so.

I recall now looking back and thinking of some of the things that the angels have told me previously regarding what I now consider to be my natural gift – that from early childhood onwards I have been able to clearly see and hear angels and clearly hear and see spirits – but it was only in adult life that I truly realised that this gift was not necessarily experienced by many people at all. Most people on a spiritual path need to learn some form of mediation in order to quieten down their busy minds, relax their bodies and mind, in order to make contact with angels and spirits.

I do consider myself to be truly blessed and privileged in not needing to do this in order to contact angels and spirits and to this day I do not know why this is the case for me specifically. I expect there are similar people like myself who see a whole range of angels and spirits whatever state their mind is in, but I have not personally come across those as yet. This is in no way meant as an egotistical statement; it is a statement of fact that I am recording within this book.

I continued with the teachings that I was now experiencing and that I would now be obtaining within the next few years, and it would be my fervent intention, and indeed destiny, to pass on as many of those teachings as possible to as many people as possible. There are literally millions of people worldwide who are following a spiritual path, either knowingly or unknowingly, and anything that I have ever learnt from the angels and spirit I see as my privilege to be able to pass on to as many people as possible who would wish to avail themselves to the teachings. This will be covered in much more detail later within this book.

As well as learning all about chakras and meditation techniques, I also learnt formally about the higher and the lower self. For ease of simplicity, I like to view my lower self as my head-mind, my ego-mind, my business mind, my day-to-day mind, whereas the higher self I see as being deep within my stomach, with a strong connection to my heart. This lower stomach area and the heart area is the part of the human body that can truly feel the vibration of angels. When one carries out a meditation and truly disengages the head-mind and allows the heart to fully open, this gets the human body into a tranquil state, which in essence raises the vibration of the human being, preparing us for contact from the spirit world.

The angels had told me many times about the vibration of a human being. They had told me that the gravity on earth is very dense and the human vibration therefore has to be relatively heavy in order to ground ourselves. Every living being, every living organism, has a vibration of some form or another. Again, for simplicity, it is best to look at the human vibration as being rather dense and rather thick, whereas the vibration of angels, spirit and elementals is very light. That is why when the human being truly learns to meditate, our vibration rises and that, coupled with the angel or spirit lowering their vibration, enables us to meet. In essence, it is the veil that is between our two worlds. The more we can do to raise our vibration, the more we can do to make our lives tranquil; the more we can do to live from our heart as opposed to our head, then the more we can open the veil between our two worlds and meet the wonders that reside in the world of spirit.

In those early months, another of the areas I received some form of training in surrounded grounding and protection. When you deal with angels, there is no need at all for any form of protection because angels always come from the highest good. They come from spiritual realms of the highest order and bring with them pure love, and none of us ever have the need to protect ourselves from the energies and advice that angels bring with them. What I must stress, however, is that there is a significant need for protection when you deal with other spiritual beings outside of the angelic realms. This particularly applies to any form of human spirits.

The importance of grounding also cannot be overstated. When somebody is first proceeding along the spiritual path and starts to carry out meditation techniques and attends any form of meditation, either singularly or in a group environment, it is vitally important to make sure that following the meditation, suitable grounding is carried out. Put simply, after any meditation work, which would generally be carried out while sitting upright in a chair – or on some occasions while lying down either on a bed or on the floor – you should always make sure that you are grounded before carrying on with your daily activities. I find a simple way to do this is to sit on a chair, making sure I am sitting upright, and have my feet firmly placed on the floor. I then close my eyes and imagine roots actually coming out from beneath my feet, like tree roots would, and imagine these roots going deep into the ground, going deeper and deeper through the layers of earth until they reach the earth's core, and then I imagine those roots encircling themselves within the earth's core and I sit there for a few minutes, visualising this. Following on from that, I generally then just visualise myself standing in a field, standing next to a beautiful oak tree and then I imagine myself touching the bark of the oak tree while still ensuring that the roots coming out from beneath my feet have gone deep into the earth's core. When I feel that I have grounded myself sufficiently, I gently open my eyes and have a stretch, sit there for a minute or two and then make my way to the nearest possible chocolate bar!

One of the other things that I studied in these early months was reiki, which is a form of hands-on healing (although it can be hands-off healing, and is a superb vehicle for sending distant healing). I went to two different reiki master teachers over these couple of years and I also obtained the level of reiki master teacher at the end of my studies on this particular activity.

There are quite a few forms of reiki and the one that I was particularly drawn to was Usui reiki, which is a form of Japanese healing. I won't go into any details about my reiki experiences but I found all of these to be of great benefit and I certainly am an advocate of the tremendous benefits of reiki healing.

One other area I studied in my early months concerned elementals. I did not have any great knowledge or experience surrounding the many forms of elementals that exist within the spirit world, which also overlap with earth, but I did have some basic knowledge. What I did not appreciate in those early months was just how vast the elemental kingdom is. I will mention a mere few within this chapter, which are nothing more than the tip of a very large iceberg.

Most people would imagine elementals to cover fairies in particular, plus one or two other spiritual beings. Many people also may just see fairies and their like as being nothing other than folklore. Well, having now had considerable first-hand experience of the elemental kingdom, I can quite categorically say that fairies and their like exist, just the same as you and I exist. Once again, however, should we wish to see elementals and should we wish to work with them, then our vibration must be at the right level and our intentions must always be honourable.

Some of the many spiritual beings that I would bracket within the elemental kingdom are flower fairies, field fairies, tree spirits, wood elves, water sprites, water nymphs, water spirits, air fairies, fire fairies, salamanders and many many other such beings.

Again, this book is not meant in any way to be a teaching on this particular area but it would be remiss of me not to mention a very important point. Should you ever walk into woods or deep into a forest, take it from me, you are being watched by the many fairies that reside there. The veil between the spirit world and the earthly world is very thin in wooded areas; the vibration of the elementals is such that they readily identify with wooded areas and readily make it known of their presence. If you pull up close to a wooded area in your car, for example, the very moment you get out of your car and approach the woods, you are being scanned. Elementals have an incredible ability to scan human beings immediately. They scan us to understand our intentions. Are our intentions honourable? Are we going to enter those woods to experience the beauty of nature and to walk in such a way that we do not disturb the very beauty that is before us, or are we one of those people that throw litter into the woods and do nothing to help the environment? You cannot fool elementals; they know immediately what your intentions are and they measure that from the intentions that emanate from your heart. You cannot fool them by thinking something differently in your head.

There are many forms of elementals that are only too happy to work with human beings on environmental projects. As long as your intentions are honourable, as long as what you are doing is for the highest good, then you can always call upon elementals to assist you.

In closing on this particular point, it would also be rather remiss of me not to mention that there are some forms of elementals that are very – and how shall I say this – troublesome, to say the least. I have had some elementals attach themselves to me without me necessarily being aware of this, and in essence I had brought the elemental into my house, where they have not exactly wreaked havoc with their mischievous nature, but they have done all sorts of naughty things!

The Leap of Faith

During the latter half of 2003 and the early part of 2004, I was still not sure of the exact path I was going to follow in terms of spirituality. I really enjoyed performing reiki healing on both animals and humans, but I still felt a deep inner calling for a totally different path. I was not sure what that path was to be so I decided to pursue other forms of spiritual teaching. I then enrolled in an eighteen-month course relating to psychic and spiritual healing. This was a very in-depth and the course consisted of attending two evenings a week, as well as some interim work in-between classes regarding paperwork and other administration tasks.

I really enjoyed the psychic and spiritual healing classes and, at the end of the eighteen-month period, I qualified as a psychic and spiritual healer under the auspices of the school that I attended. I knew for the majority of my adult life that I had healing ability, and the angels used me as a vehicle for this on many occasions, but I was still quite pleased to have this certified from an officially recognised teaching school. I carried out many sessions of voluntary healing, attending charitable healing clinics where members of the public could receive psychic and spiritual healing free of charge. I also carried out private healing on many individuals who approached me to receive such a service. It was my utmost pleasure to perform this role.

While carrying out the vast majority of the psychic and spiritual healing that I conducted, I always used the methods and techniques that I had been trained in during my eighteen-month course. On some occasions, however, I also asked for the assistance of the angels when I felt that it was appropriate to do so. I specifically used to ask Archangel Raphael to join me in carrying out healing and he was always delighted to do so. On some occasions when I asked Archangel Raphael to assist me in any particular healing, where I felt his presence was required, his arrival was always preceded with the room where I carried out the healing being basked in a dark green light. I knew that this green light was the vibration Archangel Raphael operated on and, sure enough, within just a few moments of me asking for this presence, the green light was followed by the arrival of Archangel Raphael himself.

I have said previously that angels are androgynous and they can present themselves either in male or female form but I have only ever seen Archangel Raphael as a male presence. His power, especially in relation to healing, is considerable. On some occasions, I have stood back from the client that I have been healing and just stood in awe, watching Archangel Raphael and his band of healing angels perform their work. He often calls upon the angels of purification to assist him when he is carrying out his healing work and on many occasions I have seen this in action. I can best describe the angels of purification as minute balls of light. They weave around the client, who generally is either sitting down or lying down, like a shoal of fish going all around the body of the client. They move in all sorts of directions, up and down, in and out, side to side, and generally always perform what looks like a rhythmic dance. As one angel of purification moves, so do all the others and it would be impossible to count the number while they are doing their purification work. I would estimate it to be in the low thousands.

Once the angels of purification have carried out their role, they gently vanish into the green light that would still be illuminating the room where the healing was carried out. Archangel Raphael then generally takes a step or two forward to be a little bit closer to the client and he places his arms open wide above the body of the client. I used to watch in sheer wonder at the energy that would flow through his hands into the client. On many occasions, this would be targeted on one particular area, for example, the stomach or the head, depending on the issue that the client presented.

While this was being carried out, the client would often drift into a deep trance-like state, almost as though they were asleep, in total readiness to receive the healing power of Archangel Raphael. When he finishes his work, Archangel Raphael often looks in my direction, smiling at me, and then starts to fade away, followed imminently by the dark green haze, which would have still illuminated the room. At that stage, I then move back closer to the client and carry on with the hands-on healing that I do.

The clients would always feel significant benefit from having had an archangel present during their healing session and I have many testimonials that have been verbally fed back to me but I will not go into this within this book, as I consider these to be private between the client, myself and the angels.

During some of the more what I will refer to as routine sessions of psychic and spiritual healing that I conducted, I was often accompanied by the spirit of a Victorian doctor. He was always dressed in a white shirt, dark trousers and shiny black shoes. He was about five foot nine inches tall and he told me his name was Edward. He said he was a doctor in Victorian times and he had chosen to come back almost in the capacity of a spirit guide to assist me in the healing work that I am undertaking. It was always an absolute pleasure to have Edward join me in the sessions that he chose to be present at. I still see him to this day. He is a very humorous man and always attends carrying a leather doctor's bag, which he always opens to lay out his instruments on a table. I always see this psychically by clairvoyant vision but I have also seen him on many occasions through 'normal' vision.

Jackie was now well involved in her animal healing work and she attended a foundation school to learn to become an animal healer. She was, and is, fantastic at this. Jackie has a natural empathy with animals and you can tell every time Jackie is within the presence of an animal that she has a heartfelt connection to them. I am sure that if Jackie could have had an ideal job, it would have been a crewmate on Noah's Ark!

I also carried out some sessions of animal healing and took great pleasure in doing this, but again I still felt that this was not my natural calling. I was giving psychic and spiritual healing to many people, I was giving reiki healing to many people, I was also carrying out the odd element of animal healing, but deep within me, I just knew there was something much more fundamental that I needed to be doing. At this stage, I had no idea what that was.

Jackie and I found it quite tough financially, having had to give up a big salary with Royal Mail and losing all of the benefits that that brought. We were finding it much tougher to survive, and some months we were really living on the breadline. I knew, however, that I still had to just follow the spiritual path and see where that took me.

On one particular day, I was talking in length to Chrystal, saying that I was still really confused as to what I needed to do next. I told Chrystal that I was enjoying all of the healing work that I was carrying out and that I was enjoying all of the courses that I had attended, but I still felt that I was a fish out of water and there was something more that I needed to do. I told her that the deep yearning within me, which I referred to as a calling, was growing stronger by the day.

Chrystal empathised with that comment and said that she fully understood what I was expressing but that I needed to learn patience. I told Chrystal that Jackie and I were finding it much tougher to survive, having lost the benefits of my Royal Mail position, and Jackie was once again returning to work in order to supplement the family income.

It is clear and obvious that a spiritual path, while providing massive satisfaction from a heartfelt point of view, generally could not possibly pay for the material things that most humans desire. Certainly, from Jackie's and my perspective, we were quite happy just to remain in our house and lead a much more simple life; we did not ask for much and as long as we could pay all of our bills and put food on the table, we were happy with that. We had no excessive demands whatsoever. As long as we could both survive and Jackie could carry on with her animal healing work and I could carry on with my spiritual path, we were very content with that. And to this day, I pass on my grateful thanks to the angels for all that I have, all that I have been and all that I will be, as I know deep within my heart that without the angels, I would be nothing.

I saw Chrystal almost every day during this period in 2003 and 2004 and often used to ask her advice as to what I needed to do next. I was always met by the same smile and the same knowing look that meant I needed to follow my path and choose the things that I felt were right for me. In later years, I learnt the benefit of this, as it made me much more discerning as to which training and teachings were of the highest good and which were not. I suppose it is like going out for a meal: there are some restaurants that you like and some that you do not like, there are some meals that you like and some meals that you do not like, but generally you need to have tried it all in order to form an opinion. And the same can be said for a spiritual path: having such a wide variety of teachings and teachers during my formative years of development has enabled me to understand the value of those teachers that are truly world-class.

On one particular day, and by now this must have been in the spring of 2004, I was sitting at home talking to Chrystal about all sorts of issues that I was facing at the time. Instantaneously, on this day Bella and Amhiel arrived to join Chrystal. I always so love seeing the trio of angels together; their energies bond so well and blend so well. Amhiel, with his protective male presence, supported by Bella, with her loving supportive energy, and Chrystal, with her gentle nudging energy, all blend so well and appear complementary.

Amhiel stood forward and asked me if I felt protected in the courses that I was attending. I was a little surprised by this question but I answered it honestly by saying that generally I felt protected in most of the courses that I attended, although there were some occasions when I felt unease. Amhiel asked me to ensure that I asked Archangel Michael to surround me in a purple shield of protection on any occasion where I felt such unease. I thanked him for this and said that I would do exactly that. I also asked Amhiel if he was aware of the Native American spirit guide that I had seen since childhood and still see to this day.

This spirit guide always presents himself to me sitting on a white and black horse and he always holds a spear above his head in his right hand. There are feathers draping off the spear and covering its entire length. On one of the many occasions that I have spoken to this Native American, he has told me that his name is Little Wolf and he is a member of the Sioux tribe. His primary role is to create a protection ring around me and this is particularly useful when I carry out any mediumship-type work.

Amhiel told me that he was well aware of the spirit guides that come into and out of my life at various stages of my earthly existence and Amhiel reminded me that, whereas spirit guides fluctuate in and out of your life, your guardian angels are with you in this lifetime, in any previous lifetime and in any future lifetime.

Chrystal and Amhiel took a couple of paces back and gently vanished into the ether. Bella stayed on and we must have spoken for at least an hour on a wide variety of subjects. I particularly said to Bella some of the things that I had said to Chrystal, inasmuch as I was looking for more guidance on the next steps I should take on my spiritual path. Bella smiled at this, much the same as Chrystal always did, and reminded me that I needed to take the life choices that I felt were right for me. This is the way that I would learn the lessons that needed to be learnt in order to supplement my future teaching.

I said to Bella that I recognised this but I still would appreciate some prompt as to some particular course that the angels felt I needed to go on. Bella asked me to show patience. She spoke about an archangel called Archangel Jophiel and one of the attributes that this archangel can bring to you is patience. I smiled at that myself and said to Bella I would need that in bucketloads. Bella reminded me of the need to be discerning and that this would come by attending a whole variety of workshops and classes and this is the way that I would learn the necessary lessons. Bella told me just to follow my heart and to attend the functions or events that I felt were proper for me. She asked me to feel the courses, not just to think of them in my head, but to actually feel them in my heart. I thanked Bella for that and with that she also gently stood back and started to fade away.

At that moment, I decided not to give much further thought to the next course or events that I would attend and just wait to see what happened. It was perhaps early in 2004 that I found myself once again looking on the internet at various spiritual courses when I came across an advert that was talking about a lady from California in the USA called Doreen Virtue. The article said that Doreen had been working with angels for most of her adult life and was coming to the UK to run a series of classes and workshops in London.

There was one particular workshop that I liked the look of and it was mainly aimed at making a better connection with your guardian angel. While I certainly did not need any improvement in my connection with my particular guardian angels, especially the trio of angels, I felt heavily drawn to attend this one-day workshop, so almost without any hesitation at all, I applied to go to the one-day workshop, duly paid my money for the ticket and began looking forward to attending the event, which was in the spring of 2004. I felt pleased that I had done this, and thinking back to what Bella had told me in respect of 'feeling the course' as opposed to just 'thinking' about the course, I really felt drawn to this particular event.

Approximately a couple of weeks before attending the course, a miraculous thing happened to me one night. I was fast asleep in bed when I was woken up by the presence of somebody standing next to me. I opened my eyes and could clearly see an angel standing before me. This particular angel certainly was about eight feet tall and had the most beautiful golden wings. The angel beckoned to me to follow her. She looked at me lovingly and gestured to me to get out of the bed and to walk towards her; by this time she had taken a few steps back. I instantly knew that I needed to get out of bed and duly did so.

I must have taken about three steps towards the angel when I suddenly realised that I was no longer in my bedroom. I was in the most brilliant white light that one could ever perceive. The brightness and starkness of the white light was a sight to behold. I was almost blinded by the intensity of this light. I could not see the angel; I could not see anything other than a brilliant white light. After a few moments, my eyes must have adjusted a bit as I started to make out certain shapes that were in front of me. The white light was still as bright as ever and I could vaguely see movement in front of me. I tried to clear my eyes and adjust my focus to see what was happening.

With that, I could see the angel that had previously been in my bedroom. She smiled at me and then totally vanished. It was then that I realised I was standing in the middle of a large circle, which in human dimensions must have been something like three hundred feet in diameter. Around the edge of the entire circle were large stone pillars and these pillars just went high up into the air as individual stone columns. I have no idea how many stone columns there were but I would estimate there to be at least fifty. I looked at the pillars and looked upwards, and again they must have been at least one hundred feet in earthly height, and on the top of every pillar I could see there was what looked like a stone statue of a human being. I looked at many of the stone figures on top of the pillars in sheer wonder and awe. I was amazed at what I was seeing and not for one moment did I feel any fear or any apprehension at all. In fact, I was not even thinking of where I was or how I had left my bedroom or anything of that ilk; I was just standing there in open-mouthed amazement.

I became aware that at the top of one particular pillar, one of the stone figures began to move. I was heavily surprised to see this. I looked up at this particular figure and it was a figure of a man who did not have much hair; he had some around the back of his head and on the sides, but a bald pate. It was an incredible sight, bearing in mind that I thought all of these figures were indeed made of stone, which is just what the pillar looked like. With that, the stone figure that was moving suddenly looked at me intently. I looked back at him just as intently. He stepped off of the pillar, and rather than falling to the ground as one would expect, he gently drifted down and down to become much closer to myself. Before he reached ground level, he must have been about six feet away from me when suddenly I felt myself engulfed in this incredible feeling of love and compassion. Words could not describe the depth of this feeling. It would be rather remiss of me to continue to call this person a stone figure. He indeed looked like he was made of stone, but he had movement just the same as you and I. While I was engulfed by what I will now call his aura, he said nothing to me; he just looked at me and I looked back at him.

I have no idea how long I was then standing in this position, surrounded by this love and compassion, but after a while the stone figure gently started to float back up towards the top of the pillar and then became rooted in his original position, just like all of the other stone figures on the other surrounding pillars.

I felt incredible, I felt euphoric, but I had no idea at all about what I had just witnessed. With that, I noticed coming out of the distance was the angel that had led me to this wonderful place. She moved towards me and beckoned me to walk towards her also. I must have only taken one step forward when suddenly I was standing next to her, but this time I was in my bedroom standing next to her, where this incredible journey had begun. She smiled at me and intuitively I knew that I just needed to get back into my bed and lie down: this I duly did. The angel took another couple of paces towards me and put her right hand on my forehead. I looked at her and she looked at me and gently she just started to vanish. I was wide awake. I knew this was not a dream. I know this was not a dream. What I had experienced certainly could not be rationalised or explained but I know that it happened exactly as I have said here.

When I woke up the following morning, I was a little disorientated and felt quite considerably light-headed. I decided just to have an easy day that day, not do any research about spiritual courses, and just do some of the other material things that one does on a day off. I could not help thinking about what had happened the previous night. The sheer presence of that stone circle, the pillars and the stone figures on the top was magnificent. I have revisited that place on many other occasions since that day and I am still at a total loss to explain what it is or where it is. I have asked the angels various questions surrounding this but generally their only response is to smile at me and to say just to experience the situation and not to analyse the position. I have at last taken that advice on board.

Later on that particular day, however, I was just sitting on my settee in the lounge, still thinking about what had happened the previous night, when Chrystal appeared to my right-hand side. Her energy was different on this occasion. It seemed much more electric than normal; she seemed almost as though she was in a bit of a rush, which I know could not possibly be the case for angels, but her aura and her energy did feel different.

I immediately asked Chrystal whether there was anything the matter, which looking back now must have been a terribly foolish question of a human being to ask an angel. Chrystal asked me whether I was ready to attend the workshop that would now be held in a couple of weeks' time in London with Doreen Virtue. I said that I was immensely looking forward to the workshop, and while I did not need any reinforcement of my connection with guardian angels, I just felt strangely drawn to attend the event.

Chrystal complimented me on feeling this and said that I was making a huge stride forward in attending this particular course, as it would be the gateway to many wonderful things that would now be happening for me in my work with angels and spirit guides. Chrystal then asked me to sit upright on the settee that I was sitting on, to close my eyes and just breathe in a relaxed manner. I did not question this at all – I just did exactly what Chrystal said. With that, I felt the most incredible pressure enter the room. It was as though I was in a pressure chamber, almost like a diver must feel when they go into pressurised containers. I must admit I was a little worried by this and Chrystal must have picked this up by thought immediately because she said that I just needed to stay exactly where I was and continue to breathe deeply.

I could see a variety of colours all around me, even though my eyes were closed. I could clearly see the colours vibrating around my body. I then started to see the most incredible clairvoyant visions. I saw a whole pride of lions. My eyes were still closed but clairvoyantly, and with great clarity, I could see a pride of lions. It was as though they were walking on the African plains, the open savannah. There must have been at least twenty of these lions. They all looked as though they were lionesses and there were about five or six cubs gently trotting along behind the lionesses. I looked at this in great amazement.

While clairvoyantly looking at the beautiful pride of lions, I noticed that there was one lioness that was behind all of the others. She must have been about twenty yards behind the rest of the pride and I noticed that she turned her head, almost as though she was looking at me. I was fascinated by what I was seeing and I knew that, for whatever reason, Chrystal had engineered this for me to see this vision. This last lioness at the back of the pride had the most beautiful face, and she started to let out the noise that a lioness does when she is calling her young or the rest of the pride. It was a deep grumbling noise. Amazingly, I could even see the noise vibration coming out of the lioness's mouth as this grumbling noise was made. It was exactly the same as seeing ripples in a pond if you threw a stone into the water. The vibration of this deep groan was vibrating through my entire body.

I was still looking intently at this lioness when suddenly the vision vanished completely. Everything that I was looking at vanished and all I could see was a pale pink colour before my eyes. I started to feel, however, incredible strength flowing through my body. It was as though I was picking up the lioness's courage: her bravery, her strength, her fortitude was vibrating through my entire body. It was at this moment that Chrystal asked me to open my eyes and that is exactly what I did.

I was met by the most incredible sight. There standing before me was a most beautiful angel. She was covered in a pink light that illuminated the entire room. She was much bigger than Chrystal, much taller, her wings much brighter and lighter than Chrystal's and her hair, which was long and flowing and wavy, radiated a deep colour of gold. I noticed that this angel had something in her hands, which was flickering light. Initially it was hard for me to make out what this was. It looked like a large piece of stone and was a mixture of pink and white and it almost seemed to be illuminated as the light was flickering on it, within it and around it.

I looked at this angel and she in turn looked at me. She said nothing, I said nothing and Chrystal said nothing. The angel took a step towards me and I intuitively felt the need to lean forward. At this stage, she spoke in a very authoritative voice and asked me to open my palms and to place my hands before her. I did this instantaneously and the angel placed what she was holding in the palms of my hands. She told me that she was presenting me with a piece of angel rose quartz crystal. At the time, I did not have any real knowledge of crystals but I was grateful to receive this from the angel.

Just as she placed it into my hands, it literally vanished, as though my hands had absorbed the crystal that the angel had given me. I found this to be incredible and I looked at Chrystal, who at that stage was smiling at me, immediately picking up on me yet again analysing something as opposed to just receiving it with love.

The other angel then said to me something that I will always remember, something that meant a lot to me at the time, but something that was going to mean even more to me later on. She said to me that the angels were pleased that I was about to undertake some more direct angel training. She was pleased that I was attending a one-day workshop and she said that that would lead on to a more intense series of events that would enable me to have the full list of things that the angels wanted me to have in order to carry out what she described as 'teachings in the way of the angels'.

She said to me that she would introduce herself to me now and that her name was Ariel. She said she was an angel who would work with me on many of the angel teachings that I would be undertaking. She said that she would always be there for me, as were my trio of angels; she would be there when it was appropriate for her to be there, to assist in the teachings of the angels. She said to me that Chrystal had shown me the vision of the lions and the beautiful pride as a precursor to me meeting the angel herself. She said that she would constantly show me visions of lions and lionesses and it was that that would enable me to understand who I was working with at the time. I truly felt grateful for everything that the angel Ariel said.

With that, Ariel started to fade away and the pink light went with her as she left the room. I was then alone with Chrystal and I sat back on the settee, feeling almost in shock at the depth of what had just happened. I said to Chrystal I felt the presence of the angel even before she entered the room and I did not ask Chrystal this but Chrystal said to me that what I had just been exposed to was the presence of an archangel. I was a little bit surprised by this, as even though previously I had worked quite closely with Archangel Michael and Archangel Raphael, this was the first real time that I had worked closely with another archangel.

Chrystal said that Archangel Ariel, whose name means 'Lioness of God', has many attributes that she would be bringing to help in my angel teachings. She said that she would be bringing bravery and courage to get across some of the hard-hitting messages that the angels would need put across and she also said that Archangel Ariel has a very strong link with the animal kingdom and can assist greatly in any animal healing. This would certainly explain the vision of the lionesses I saw, and in particular the lioness that was about twenty yards behind the rest of the pride, who was looking at me intently; she must have been looking at me through the eyes of an archangel.

I truly felt blessed having witnessed everything that I had witnessed. I thanked Chrystal for this. Chrystal said that there was no need for thanks; all I needed to do was to feel everything that the angels were doing for me. I truly felt an incredible gratitude to Chrystal and indeed Archangel Ariel for the visit.

Before leaving, Chrystal said something to me that at the time had little meaning and did not appear to have a great deal of relevance, but later on, when I was to carry out my own angel teachings by running my own angel workshops, I realised the relevance of the phrase that she was about to give me. She said that Archangel Ariel had spoken separately to Chrystal and had a message for me, one that she did not give me herself but she did say to Chrystal. The message was, 'Have faith, leap and we leap with you.'

This was an incredibly touching comment by Chrystal, and even though at the time I did not know the relevance, I found the words to be beautiful. The way that Chrystal said the words, the way they came directly from the heart of angels, really vibrated through my entire body. 'Have faith, leap and we leap with you.'

My Major Breakthrough

It was with great excitement that I attended the one-day workshop held by Doreen Virtue in London. There must have been over 700 people there and the atmosphere was electric. Doreen came on to the stage at the beginning of the workshop, almost looking like an angel. She had this long, flowing purple gown on and she gracefully walked on to the stage. You could tell immediately that she was indeed a truly gifted medium and angel practitioner. She introduced herself and quickly made everybody in the audience feel very relaxed.

The day consisted of some meditations and some formal teachings, as well as a few readings that Doreen gave to members of the audience. I could see all sorts of angels present in the room throughout the workshop and indeed it was a great honour to be in the atmosphere that Doreen and the angels generated. I had a fabulous day and while I was travelling back home, I was thinking about where this particular workshop would lead.

It was clear to me that the angels wanted me to attend this one-day workshop but what was not clear to me is what my next steps were to be. I tried so hard to exhibit the patience that the angels had asked me to and I also tried hard to just feel and enjoy the events without necessarily analysing them either before, during or after. What followed on from this workshop, though, was indeed truly awesome. Over the next week or so, I researched on the internet everything there was regarding Doreen Virtue and the events that she ran. I found that in October 2004 she intended to run a workshop in Laguna Beach, California, which was a one-week workshop, and those attending, providing they met the qualifying standard, would finish the course with the formal certification of angel therapy practitioner (ATP).

Doreen's website had a whole host of events listed on it and one thing that I was particularly drawn to was the chat room she had for all certified ATPs. I was convinced that that was the path I now needed to follow. While I could see and talk to angels regularly, I felt it would be useful for me to go for the ATP certification, in order to better understand the way that I needed to teach others to achieve likewise. While I had been truly blessed with the gift of being able to see angels with such clarity, it was now abundantly clear to me that there were many other people who would like the ability to do the same, but just did not have the awareness of how to achieve that position.

I spoke to Jackie about this and she was her normal supportive self. Irrespective of the cost, Jackie has always supported me in my spiritual ventures and yet again she was a rock, saying to me that, irrespective of the cost, if I felt drawn to attend the ATP course in October 2004, then I should book the ticket. In fact, it was Jackie who then went on the internet and actually booked me the tickets to attend the ATP course and she also booked the accommodation and my flights. It puts me in mind of that phrase they say at the end of most films, 'without whose help, this would not have been possible'. This certainly applies to Jackie's help for me.

Between my one-day workshop in London and the formal ATP event in Laguna Beach, I studied everything there was on Doreen Virtue. I read most of her books, of which there are many, and I bought some of her angel oracle cards, which I knew I would need on the ATP course itself. I found the use of angel and archangel oracle cards initially to be quite difficult, because I just speak to the angels as I see them – they have certainly never needed to use implements such as cards in order to make contact with me; but I thought it would be of use in understanding how these cards worked, as I was well aware that there are many people who receive great support by using oracle cards and suchlike and get their messages from the angels via this route.

The day of the ATP course duly arrived and it was with great excitement that I flew out from London Heathrow to Los Angeles International Airport. I was then due to connect with a small flight from Los Angeles to Orange County. There was then a short bus ride from Orange County Airport to the hotel in Laguna Beach, California.

Well, I can certainly say that Laguna Beach is exactly as one would imagine. It was almost a *Baywatch*-type place, with long golden beaches and beautiful weather. I can easily understand why Doreen Virtue chose to hold her workshops there, as well as also personally live in this wonderful place.

I won't necessarily go into any great detail of the ATP course but suffice it to say the whole week was one of incredible energy and fantastic sights and sounds. I saw literally thousands of angels and spirits during the week and the angels themselves so love attending events such as this, because all of those attending have goodness in their heart and generally are attending for the right reasons, that reason being to work with and for angels for the greater good of humanity and the earth. It was my pleasure to attend the event and I must record my grateful thanks for everything that Doreen taught during the week, as much of it enabled me to cement my own personal teachings to enable me to run the workshops that I did following on from the Laguna Beach event.

There are a few things, however, that I would like to record that arose during the ATP week. I met some wonderful people and shared some wonderful experiences with them during the course. One of the strangest things that happened to me at the course did not relate to angels or spirits in any way at all. I remember being in my hotel room one evening; it must have been fairly late because I had just completed the administration work that we had to hand in every morning at course registration. I was about to go to bed, got myself ready and turned the light off.

Just as I got into the bed, I was aware of something touching the end of the bed. The room was dimly lit but there was enough light for me to see that there was indeed something on the end of the bed. I immediately knew that this was spiritual rather than specifically physical so I did not feel any fear. What I saw was incredibly surprising to me at the time and even now I am still a little surprised at what I witnessed. On the end of the bed was an animal, which was in spirit form. I knew that it was in spirit form as opposed to being a living animal, but even though I knew that, I was still relatively surprised at what I was seeing. By this stage, the entire animal had stood on the bed and it would best be described as the size of an anteater, but with different physical characteristics. This spirit animal was on the end of the bed for quite a few minutes and made a strange noise as well as carrying out some strange actions. Within a matter of minutes, it had gone as quickly as it had arrived. It was later on in life that I was to be told that many humans have animal spirits connected to them and some of these animal spirits are not necessarily of an earthly animal. I have no idea where this animal came from, but I can clearly say the spiritual animal, as it was, was certainly not from the planet earth.

I mentioned this to a couple of people the following day on the ATP course and both of them had their version of what it was that I had experienced the night before. Both did relate to animal spirits and the presence thereof, though.

The ATP course consisted of many fabulous things, as we were taught by the angels themselves, supported by Doreen Virtue, although some people may well see it as Doreen Virtue supported by the angels! Either way, the course itself was fantastic. We were taught all manner of things, many of which would stand me in great stead when I was to hold my own workshops and carry out my own spiritual teachings. Some of the things particularly relevant to angel workshop training surrounded angel card readings, automatic writing, angel meditations, how to meet your guardian angel, how to increase your clairvoyant ability, how to increase your clairaudient ability, how to increase your clairsentient ability, how to increase your claircognisant ability, grounding and protection techniques, plus many more similar and related topics. I found every topic to be of use and there was always something to learn and always something to see during every session held at the ATP course.

On the penultimate night of the ATP course, I was lying in bed, just thinking of how sad I would be to finish the course, and while I was greatly looking forward to going home, having missed my wife and family, I would also be sad to leave behind such a wonderful, loving energy.

Bella must have picked up on this because she was the first of the trio of angels to appear on that particular night. Bella sat on the end of the bed and spoke to me at some length regarding the things I had learnt. She once again, and I noticed this within her at the time, as she kept stressing this point, advised that I needed to make sure that I was feeling the emotion of all of the topics that I was being taught, as well as learning the techniques that were being displayed. I said to Bella that it would be impossible not to feel the emotion of an ATP course just by being present in the surroundings that we were in, where many likeminded people were present along with their own guardian angels. One could not fail to be touched.

Bella said to me that my business mind and all of my business acumen would stand me in good stead for running spiritual courses, and what the angels were doing to me now was opening my heart chakra so that I could truly feel the energy and the vibration associated with many of the angel teachings. Bella said to me that I would come across literally hundreds of people who would benefit from the teachings I would deliver on behalf of the angels, and the vast majority of these would not be in their head-mind at all; in fact, nearly all of them would be in their heart and would really feel the teachings that I would deliver, as well as feel the angels that would be all about them during the training sessions.

Bella said to me that I would be exposed to some words that wise shamans have used in the past. She reminded me of how I felt every time I saw Little Wolf, my wonderful Native American guide, and how Little Wolf's energy was one of earthly connection, spiritual connection and with a strong protection presence. Bella told me that at one of the angel workshops that I would be running, I would be asked to quote something that some people are aware of, but that all of humanity would do well to remind themselves.

Bella said that the majority of the human race had lost sight of their main reason for being. She said that every single human being, and indeed every living organism, has a part of 'the source' within them. Whether you see this as a creator, whether you see this as God, whether you see this in whatever way suits your own religious or otherwise beliefs, every single person and every single soul has a part of that original creation within them. Bella said that the major business corporations and the major drug companies had contributed to mankind losing its way. We have forgotten the simplicity of life, we have forgotten that love is all, and that everything else is an illusion. Bella asked me to remember something that she then went on to say. She said that in the ancient days if you visited a Native American shaman and asked for any form of healing, the shaman would ask you four questions prior to giving that healing:

- When did you stop singing?
- When did you stop dancing?
- When did you stop being enchanted by stories?
- When did you stop listening to the sweet sound of silence?

Bella recited these four shaman questions in such a way that I couldn't fail to be touched by the sheer simplicity and the sheer beauty of the words that she chose. It is my delight to pass these on. From a coincidental basis, or should I say a synchronicity basis, Doreen Virtue's husband, a man called Steven, also has a very strong link with Native American culture, and power animals in particular. 'Power animals' is a term that is used to describe the presence of spirit animals that are on earth to help mankind.

During one of the evening sessions at the ATP course, Steven held a Native American ceremony, where he conjured up all forms of animal spirits. Steven also spoke about the shaman and raised similar questions to those that Bella had told me that the shaman would ask. As I said, whether this is synchronicity or coincidental, I will leave for you to decide. All I know is what Steven said was totally accurate, and what the angels said was totally accurate, and therefore these four shaman questions really should be used by every human, to ask of themselves if their life is being led in this manner. I believe we are all too busy, too intricate and too pressured and these four shaman questions should give us the opportunity to re-evaluate our lives and perhaps slow down in all that we do and perhaps enjoy nature more, perhaps go out for walks in the woods and on hills and just breathe in the wonder of nature that is all around us.

I thanked Bella for telling me of those four shaman questions and almost instantaneously Amhiel and Chrystal arrived. It was good to see the trio of angels back together. We spoke for some time and I mentioned to Amhiel and Chrystal how much I enjoyed the words that Bella had used regarding the shaman. Amhiel said to me that at my very first angel workshop, I would also be told about the Toltec race and the four key agreements that the Toltecs used to use as a baseline for all of their actions. I had never heard of the Toltec race. I had certainly heard of Aztecs but never the Toltecs. Amhiel said to me that at my first workshop, I would be given information on a book surrounding the Toltecs, which would give greater clarity on the four agreements themselves and the relevance of this to mankind today.

Amhiel told me what those four agreements were and they were as follows:

- Be impeccable with your word.
- Take nothing personally.
- Don't make assumptions.
- Always do your best.

Amhiel explained what these actual words meant in relation to mankind. I thanked Amhiel for this but at the time did not realise the significance of the words he was saying to me. It was only later, during my first angel workshop, that what Amhiel had predicted did indeed come true. I had totally forgotten all about the four agreements when an angel appeared at my first workshop and mentioned the book that Amhiel had referred to. I'm so glad that happened as, again, the book explains the simplicity of these four agreements, and I think in conjunction with what Bella had said regarding the four shaman questions, the combination of the eight points really do encapsulate some areas that the whole human race would benefit from, just by awareness of it if nothing else.

Chrystal, who is never shy to come forward, did not say much on this particular evening; it was mainly Bella and Amhiel talking to me. Chrystal did, however, pick up when I was getting a bit tired and said that the angels would leave me as I would need to be relatively refreshed for my last day at the ATP course, which was the following day. On this occasion, they did not take a step back; they just literally vanished before my eyes.

The following day was a mixture of sheer elation and sheer sadness, elation at still being in the wonderful presence that an ATP course can deliver and the sadness of the course itself ending. There were many tearful goodbyes expressed by all of the delegates at the course and there was a lot of hugging and emotion as people said their goodbyes and made tracks on their own journeys home. People had travelled from all four corners of the globe to attend this ATP course and the angels had stressed to me that we were all beacons of light, we were all charged with angel energy, we would all always display angel light and in essence we were a continuation of the angels' main role, that of being God's messengers to deliver light into the wider world.

When I made my own way back to the UK, I was sitting on the connecting flight at Orange County Airport waiting for the short journey to Los Angeles International Airport with about ten other people. It was a very small charter plane that must have only held about thirty people in total. I looked out of the window at the airport and the runway itself and my window seat was actually adjacent to one of the plane wings. I was looking out on to the wing when I saw the most incredible sight. There standing on the aeroplane wing was a leprechaun. I realise that that may seem strange and to some people it may seem totally far-fetched, but I promise you: on the aeroplane wing was a leprechaun.

He must have been about two or three feet tall, he was dressed in trousers and boots and he had a distinctive three-pointed hat on. He looked at me and smiled and lifted his hat, just as men would have done in the olden days, when a gentleman would have raised his hat to ladies. I smiled at this leprechaun and then he did something which still makes me chuckle to this day: he bent down as though he was an air traffic controller, working on the deck of an aircraft carrier, and he pointed his two hands forward as if to say to the pilot, start your engines and make your way. I smiled at this and simultaneously the aircraft did indeed start its engines. A moment or two later, the aircraft started to move slowly towards the runway and, with that, the leprechaun jumped off of the wing. I never saw him again.

I had seen many things previous to this in relation to angels and guides and spirits in general, but the ATP course was a major breakthrough in my removing some of the self-imposed barriers and beliefs that I had in relation to all manners of other spiritual things. I can now categorically say that elementals exist, fairies exist, power animals exist and other extraterrestrial spirit forms exist. It is only our personal belief systems that provide a boundary to this. All I know is that if we truly opened our minds, if we truly opened our hearts, if we truly removed all of our own self-imposed barriers and beliefs, then the spirit world that is out there, the world that is adjacent to our own world, could be a gateway for all sorts of wonderful things.

I promised myself that from that moment on, I would never again have a barrier to the spirit world. I would never again have doubts as to what does exist and what does not exist. All I have seen to date is just the tip of an iceberg; there are other, many other, wonderful things that exist in the spirit world that I hope one day the whole of the human race will be able to better and more fully understand.

By the time I returned home to the UK, I was still infused with all of the teachings that I had received and there was so much to tell Jackie about, so much for me to remember and so much for me to enjoy. I came back enthused. I had absolutely no doubt whatsoever that I would pass on the teachings that I had received on the ATP course at the earliest possible time. I was, after all, working directly for the angels in this. There are no better employers.

As well as planning the angel workshops that I intended to run, I also looked at a wide variety of holistic fayres and psychic and spiritual fayres that were being advertised with a view to attending these so that I could pass on some of the many lessons that I had learnt. I also still had a bit of a yearning for other areas, as well as what I had been shown on the ATP course, and in the next month or so I enrolled on mediumship courses that were being held in the Lake District and where an intensive form of training in the processes, procedures and techniques surrounding the whole area of mediumship took place.

I had this insatiable thirst, this insatiable drive, to learn as much as I could on spirituality. I felt that the ATP course had given me the full coverage of everything that I could ever need in order to train people, teach people and coach people regarding angels, and of course during any angel course I ran, I would also be surrounded by the angels themselves so that I could readily pass on their messages.

My drive to attend the mediumship training was based on the need to get closer to my own spirit guides and understand how I could help other people who wanted a better contact with their spirit guides. This was something that was not fully covered at the ATP course and mediumship is therefore a different entity altogether to angel therapy. With the help of the angels, no doubt I chose wisely as to the mediumship course to attend. The course was run by a lovely, wonderful lady called Val. She came from a place of pure love; all of her teachings were delivered purely from her heart and her spiritual connection with spirit guides and spirits in general was top drawer. It was my greatest pleasure to train under her and to develop my own mediumship abilities.

I attended a beginner's and intermediate course with Val and then was invited back for a one-week diploma course, which was also to be held in the Lake District. I am pleased to say that I duly 'graduated' from the mediumship course and was certified as a medium. As mentioned previously, there is no certification needed in relation to contacting angels or spirit and spirit guides, and the certification is really there to demonstrate that you have been taught in a way where processes and procedures, especially in relation to personal protection, are duly followed.

Following on from my mediumship courses and prior to commencing the many angel workshops that I intended to run, I also attended some spirit circles. There are two types of circle that one can attend in order to contact spirit. One is called an open circle, which is usually run at spiritualist churches and anybody can attend those. Following on from the open circle, there is then the next level of circles; these are called closed circles. Attendance of closed circles is by invitation only. Generally you will be 'noticed' at an open circle and after a matter of weeks or months, depending on what is right for you and the circle itself, you may find yourself being invited to a closed circle.

I attended many closed circles, run by different people, and it was during these closed circles that I became fully appreciative of everything the angels had told me in relation to being discerning. It was clear to me that some circles were run by people that were stuck in their ego-mind, or were not working for the highest good, or were working for personal gain. But, equally, there were some circles run by people who genuinely worked for spirit and worked from their heart. I did not hang around long at any circles where they were not of the highest good, and by using the discerning ability that I had built up and by talking to my own trio of angels, I was always led to the closed circles that the circle leader and the circle attendees designed to work for the highest good. It was at these circles where my ability to contact spirit, almost by will, was enhanced considerably. Little did I know that most of the spirit rescue work that I would do later on in life would follow from the baseline I was being shown at the circles that I was attending.

I call 2004 my major breakthrough year in terms of spirituality. Having attended the ATP course in Laguna Beach and having attended the mediumship courses in the Lake District, supplemented by the many circles I attended, I knew that I was ready to really start to make considerable progress on my spiritual path. All of the building blocks were in place, all of my platforms were ready, and I was now ready to go out into the world and carry out the work that the angels had asked of me. I thought back to what Archangel Ariel had passed on to me – 'Have faith, leap and we leap with you' – and it is those words that echoed through every fibre of my being.

I then decided that I would indeed leap – leap into the world of training others on the subject of angels and spirit. I would have total trust in my heart and total love in my soul, knowing that what I was about to do was what I had committed to do prior to birth. It was what the angels wanted me to do, it was what I wanted to do, it was what my soul wanted me to do: it was, after all, my destiny.

Attending Holistic Fayres

Having returned enthused from the ATP course in Laguna Beach, I set about deciding on how I would begin to run the angel workshops that I was being led to undertake. I thought an ideal stepping stone to running my own angel workshops would be attending holistic fayres and carrying out angel readings for those who wanted them. I was a little apprehensive and nervous at the thought of this, even though I knew the angels would be there in their droves, assisting me in the accuracy of the readings that I would undertake. I had carried out many readings during the ATP course and all of the clients gave me some wonderful feedback, so obviously I knew that the readings were accurate, as the information I passed on came directly from the many angels that used to attend during the reading itself. Rolling that out, however, to paying clients was obviously a different ball game.

I looked on the internet and in local mind, body and spirit shops for the next available fayres that I could attend. I saw a fayre advertised, just a week or so away, at a place in Hampshire called Petersfield. There were also others advertised in Wickham in Hampshire, Hordean in Hampshire and at various other local sites. I immediately enrolled with the organisers of these events and organised for me to have a pitch at the event so that I could undertake the angel readings.

In the intervening week or so, prior to the first mind, body and spirit fayre that I attended as an angel card reader, I set about getting ready all of the things that I would be taking with me. I wanted to make the table that would be between myself and the client as 'angel-looking' as possible. To that end, I purchased some angel ornaments and had various light and candle effects, as well as a silk tablecloth and suchlike. I also decided that I would take two sets of angel cards with me for the readings to take place.

The angels always found this rather amusing and on many occasions they said to me, during the ATP course, I did not need the angel cards in front of me at all as they were standing in front of me themselves and would communicate directly with me. Doreen Virtue, however, had always said that having the angel cards available in some way gave support to the client and often the client would comment on the messages on the cards themselves or the pictures that were shown on the cards. Looking back now, I also find it rather amusing to consider that a client would look at the angel cards, and receive various messages and support from those cards, without realising that standing literally either to their right or to their left, or in some cases behind them, were their own personal guardian angels.

The first angel card reading that I carried out for a paying client at a mind, body and spirit fayre was a wonderful occasion. I was sitting at my angel table, looking around at the various people who were walking around the fayre, admiring the many angels that were with them. I always find that when people are congregated in an area such as a mind, body and spirit fayre or at a spiritual workshop, the angels seem to be with them in far greater numbers than in, say, a shopping precinct. In my mind, this is clearly a reflection of the energies that surround such an event and the angels find it easy to naturally gravitate to a loving environment.

While looking about at the many people milling around at the other stalls, I noticed one particular lady who had walked past my table on two or three occasions and she always seemed to be looking at the angel ornaments that I had on the table. The lady in question had a male angelic presence with her. When I first saw this particular angel, he was not fully formed; he was more a ball of light that was to the lady's right-hand side as she was walking around. I knew that it was her guardian angel but I was surprised at the lack of clarity surrounding him. He had obviously decided to not fully manifest in this particular environment.

Shortly thereafter, the lady approached my table and said that she would like an angel card reading and asked if it would be OK for me to carry that out. I smiled at the lady and asked her to take a seat, and we spoke for a few minutes on nothing in particular. I could tell that the lady was a little bit apprehensive but I am pleased to say that she was soon put at ease. She asked whether she could tell me a little bit about herself. I said that there was really no need to do this, as the angels would tell me everything that I needed to know in order to carry out the reading for her. She smiled at this and it was about this time that the male angel presence that was with her took the full shape of an angel.

He was a charming male angel with short fair hair and he was carrying a small box in his hands. I would describe the box as a small trinket-type box but at no stage did the angel open it and at no stage did he comment as to what the box represented, but I am sure it would have been something relevant to the lady who was now with me for the angel card reading. I went through the normal process that I carry out when I perform angel card readings and asked the lady to place her hands on the table so that I could gently put my hands on top of hers, so that we had a mixture of our energy. I told the lady to relax, to breathe in a relaxed way, and that I would shortly commence the angel card reading.

The reading itself was obviously personal between the lady and myself and the angels that were present, but some wonderful things were mentioned during the reading. On a number of occasions during the reading itself, the lady was in tears at some of the things that were being said. She asked me on quite a few occasions how I could have possibly known some of the specific details I had given her and I told her that I was nothing other than a channel for the angels. All of the information I would be passing on, and indeed did pass on, was pure and from the angelic realms. This applies to every single angel card reading that I ever carried out from that day to this.

I carried out about ten angel card readings at the first fayre that I attended and I was very pleased with how they all went. I did find myself getting rather tired towards the end of each of the days, as it was quite draining in those early days, holding on to the necessary concentration levels and holding on to the angelic energy that was all around. I really gave every angel card reading my all and it would be impossible not to get caught up in the emotion of many of the readings. Even though I tried to keep myself as purely a vessel for the angel messages that were coming through, when each angel card reading finished, I always felt the emotions and the different energy levels that were evident during and after the readings. This does take its toll on the human body and to experience light-headedness at that stage is normal. At the end of every individual angel card reading, and indeed at the end of every single mind, body and spirit fayre that I attended, I always thanked the angels for their help and support during the readings in question. I also asked them to continue to support and guide all of the clients who received angel card readings and to assist them all in their day-to-day lives, however it was appropriate to do so.

Over the next few months, I attended many mind, body and spirit fayres and the angels were always there in great numbers to support all of my angel card readings. I really enjoyed doing these and giving emotional support to all of the clients that presented themselves to me. Many of these clients were obviously led to me by their own guardian angels, nudging them at the appropriate time.

After a few months doing the angel card readings, I was also being nudged by Chrystal to begin carrying out the angel workshops that I needed to. This would obviously be a far greater step than just performing angel card readings at small fayres but I pledged to Chrystal that I would indeed carry out these workshops. I knew that that would follow fairly promptly and I was greatly looking forward to the day when I ran my own first angel workshop.

A few weeks after attending one particular mind, body and spirit fayre, I saw a couple of adverts for another fayre at a place called Eastleigh in Hampshire and also one for a much larger festival at Gunwharf Quays in Portsmouth. I was drawn to both of these events so I got in touch with the event organisers and duly purchased a stand at the holistic fayre in Eastleigh, as well as booking myself into the major mind, body and spirit festival that was held annually at that time in Gunwharf Quays. The contrast between these two events was staggering.

When I attended the Eastleigh fayre to carry out angel card readings, I was shocked and saddened at the energy of the hall where the fayre was being held. It was a dull, dark, depressing energy and I knew immediately that the angels would have great trouble in presenting themselves with clarity in such a hostile atmosphere. Angels naturally gravitate to a light, warm and loving energy, so the energy that I was faced with in Eastleigh would be quite difficult for them to overcome.

While at the Eastleigh event, I could tell some of the other readers that were present were not of the highest good. There was a lady on the table next to me giving psychic readings and I could clearly hear her making all sorts of claims regarding the spirit world passing her messages when clearly this was not the case. There were other things that were going on at the fayre that I will not mention here but needless to say it was clear evidence that many of the people at that particular event were working from their own egos and had no spiritual input whatsoever. Needless to say, I did not stay very long at the event and a little later on, I could hear and feel the angels contacting me, asking me to withdraw from this event. I duly did this without a moment's hesitation.

When I got home later that night, I asked the angels why they had led me to attend such an event, as it was clear that there was very little, if any, spiritual input whatsoever. Bella was the main angel that I spoke to at this time and she said that every event that I attended would be one of the lessons that I needed to learn and on this particular occasion the lesson that needed to be reinforced was my need to be even more discerning than I had hitherto been. I always took everybody at face value at a mind, body and spirit festival. I always assumed that they had the highest good of the clients at heart and I always assumed that they had strong spiritual connections themselves. The Eastleigh event gave me clear evidence that there were some people involved on the spiritual ladder, charging clients large sums of money for services that were in no way spiritual.

To this day, this saddens me greatly. There are many people out there that are looking for proof of life after death, there are many people who have lost loved ones and are seeking spiritual input and spiritual guidance, and to know that some supposed spiritual readers take advantage of these vulnerable people is a total travesty. It is the total opposite of what spirit wants to happen. True spiritual input, true angel input, is always pure, and always comes from the heart and comes from a place of love. The only person that matters is the client. All clients deserve 100-per-cent truth and 100-per-cent purity, whether it is for a paid service or not, and for the readers that are like myself, those that work for the angelic realms, it is our pleasure to pass on this accuracy and purity.

The Gunwharf event, however, was the total opposite and a complete contrast to the Eastleigh event. The mind, body and spirit festival took place over a three-day period and was truly awesome. The energies at the event when I was setting up the night before, ably assisted by Jackie, were palpable. The energies over the three days during the angel card readings were wonderful and loving. The angels were, as usual, there in great numbers and they led many people to receive the angel card readings that were necessary for them at the time to enable them to make further spiritual progress and further progress in their own human, physical life.

I also gave some lectures during my time there and these consisted of one-hour workshops to give a flavour of the angels to those who were interested. These were attended by quite large numbers of people and again it was fascinating to see the amount of guardian angels that were present during these workshops. Again, it was impossible not to be touched by the loving energy that large numbers of angels produce at events such as this.

My First Angel Workshop

Both Bella and Chrystal had been intimating to me that my first angel workshop was now approaching, and while I felt some nerves at the thought of this, this was far outweighed by the sense of excitement that I felt in passing on the many lessons that I had learnt and the teachings that I had received at my own angel therapy workshops in the USA. Jackie and I searched for a suitable venue to hold the first angel workshop and we selected a venue in Portsmouth, which was called the Universal Energy Centre. This particular venue had a loving energy around it and within, and was run by a couple of people who taught a variety of spiritual subjects. The workshop venue had reiki energy pervading through it and also had a large quantity of crystals spread throughout the building. As soon as I met the people who owned the property and after I had walked around the accommodation itself, I knew immediately that this would indeed be a fabulous place to run my first ever angel workshop. Having learnt so much on my own angel therapy course, which was held over a week, I was having some difficulty deciding how to set up my own angel workshops and I spoke to Bella about this on many occasions.

I eventually decided to set up the workshops as three individual one-day events, with the first workshop being a one-day beginner's level, a second workshop being a one-day intermediate level and the third workshop being a one-day advanced level. Each of these workshops was incremental to the preceding workshop, culminating in the advanced level as the icing on the cake to the two preceding workshops. It was my intention and my aim, and dare I say my destiny, to teach every single thing that I had been taught on my own angel therapy course in Laguna Beach, as well as teaching as much as I could of everything that I had ever learnt from the angels. It was a total privilege for me to do this and I consider myself blessed to have been given the opportunity to run these workshops.

Perhaps I should not have been too surprised but with only very limited advertising, large numbers of people were still drawn to the workshops. The reason, which should not have been a surprise to me, is that the angels will have led the right people to attend. Generally, and this applied to every venue in which I ever chose to hold workshops, numbers came to fill the available space in the accommodation. If the workshop held sixteen people, generally that is how many people would book a place on the workshop; if the workshop would hold thirty people, then that is how many people booked. There were obviously hundreds of people that the angels wanted to attend these workshops and I chose venues throughout the Hampshire area, and indeed at other venues within the UK. All of the workshops generated such love, such passion and such emotion and it was my greatest honour to be able to attend these and run these in conjunction with, and on behalf of, the angels.

There were many subjects that I put on the agendas for the workshops and some of the most important of these were angel card readings, automatic writing, the four clairs and how to increase your own clair ability, the archangels, the angel hierarchy, and so on. It may be worth giving a brief overview of some of these important topics within this book and I will do that where I feel it is appropriate to do so.

For example, the angel hierarchy. There are nine levels of angels, split into three categories within three separate hierarchies. I will list these here for clarity:

Hierarchy One: Heavenly Counsellors – Closest to the Divine Source

LEVEL ONE: SERAPHIMS – PURE LOVE TO SOURCE

- highest order of angelic hierarchy;
- highly evolved beings;
- balance movement between the planets by using sound.

Level Two: Cherubims – Guardians of Light

- second-highest order of ranking;
- guardians of light that emanate from the sun, moon and stars;
- name means 'wisdom';
- record-keepers of heaven.

Level Three: Thrones – Guardians of Planet

- third-highest ranking;
- angel of the planets;
- the earth angel is called Lady Giya.

Hierarchy Two: Heavenly Governors

Level Four: Dominians – Celestial Prefects

- fourth-ranking order of angels;
- regulators of angelic levels not as evolved as themselves;
- primary purpose to advise lower angelic groups.

Level Five: Virtues – Angels of Nature

- fifth-ranking order of angels;
- angels of nature, miracles and blessings;
- known as the 'brilliant' or 'shining' angels as they transmit beams of divine light.

Level Six: Powers – Angels of Transformation

- sixth-ranking order of angels;
- angels of transformation;
- keepers of akashic records (record of all thoughts and actions of each soul);
- overseers of birth, death and rebirth.

Hierarchy Three: Heavenly Messengers

LEVEL SEVEN: PRINCIPALITIES – OVERSEERS OF CITIES AND LARGE ORGANISATIONS

- seventh-ranking order of angels;
- overseer of cities and nations.

LEVEL EIGHT: ARCHANGELS – INDIVIDUAL POWERS/ LEADER OF ANGELS

- eighth-ranking order of angels;
- leaders of angels;
- most commonly known are Gabriel, Michael and Raphael.

LEVEL NINE: ANGELS (INCLUDING GUARDIAN ANGELS)

- ninth-ranking order of angels;
- closest to humanity;
- made up of many different angels with many different purposes;
- guardian angels are included in this category.

When I first learnt that the angels had a hierarchy, I was very surprised. I had come from an intense business background and I was rather surprised, therefore, to see a form of structure surrounding angels. Obviously, however, this is only of interest to those who want to know how angels themselves have evolved and the different levels within angelic evolution. For us as mere mortals, and human beings generally, we are only in contact with levels eight and nine, which are the archangels and guardian angels. The other levels listed above, while being of interest perhaps, do not directly interact with human beings on a day-to-day basis.

As well as having structure around the angels, there are of course lots of instances of angelic contact that have no structure whatsoever. For example, white feathers are a commonly known, what I would call, 'angel's calling card'. If you ever find yourself walking in a park or walking through the woods and you suddenly notice a white feather that really catches your eye, then this could well be a sign of the angels making contact with you. Many people get great reassurance from seeing white feathers and get great comfort in taking this as a sign that their guardian angel is near to them.

Numbers sequencing is also another form of communication that the angels sometimes use. For example, the number nine is important to the angels, as this represents the angel hierarchy, as does the number three. The angels also like the number four as a demonstration of their close proximity. The way numbers sequencing works is that you may notice the number four, or indeed the number forty-four or indeed the number four hundred and forty-four, in some of your everyday activity and if you keep noticing the same number cropping up over and over again, this can well be a demonstration that the angels are close by and trying to attract your attention for a particular reason. Try this out over a period of time and see if you start to notice the same number appearing over and over again, and if you do, you can try to find a period of stillness in your life, perhaps just before going to sleep one night, and ask the angels what it is they are trying to tell you.

Another thing that the angels use constantly is synchronicity. I refer to this as just like a domino rally in terms of angelic presence and the way that they can influence and line things up in a synchronistic way so that we become more aware of angelic presence. Some people would call some of these incidents perhaps coincidental, but I am a great believer in synchronicity.

While carrying out the first few workshops that I conducted on behalf of the angels, there were three archangels who were invariably present for the majority, if not all, of the workshop time. I did see my trio of angels on an infrequent basis during the workshops but generally they had no input in the workshop itself. The three archangels that were always present at some time or another and had great input in the way that the workshops would be run on the day, and the dialogue that would be held, were Archangel Michael, Archangel Jophiel and Archangel Ariel.

I was not at all surprised to see Archangel Michael joining every workshop because he is the archangel of protection and I always called upon him before, during and after every workshop to surround the workshop venue, and indeed to surround individual workshop attendees with a purple shield of protection during the workshops. This ensured that, from a spiritual perspective, only the highest and the best would ever get through to the workshop and that would generally be restricted to angelic presence only, as opposed to other forms of spiritual presence.

Archangel Jophiel used to attend parts of the workshop and her presence was always preceded by the workshop room developing a yellow haze. She told me that her main mission at the workshops was to illuminate the spiritual path of all of the attendees so that they would make the best possible choices in their own spiritual development. She also provided individual attendees with patience, something that is not necessarily a human virtue!

Archangel Ariel used to drift in and out of the workshops at particular times, but I've never held a workshop where Archangel Ariel was not present at some time or another. I see her main reason for being there as to provide all of the workshop attendees with courage, the courage that they would need in order to face up to the many challenges that we humans face in our normal physical day-to-day lives, and indeed the many challenges we face while forging ahead on a spiritual path. A spiritual path is never easy. It is indeed a rocky path, it can be an extremely lonely path, it can be a path that leaves you open to ridicule and criticism, but it is a path that always leads to great fulfilment and satisfaction, and it is a path that reconnects us with our inner selves. The true us, as we were meant to be.

Jackie attended almost every workshop I held in the early days, one as a workshop attendee in her own right (as she also loved the energy that was generated at the workshops), but also as my administration assistant, carrying out the many administrative tasks involved in the workshops. Again, I can safely say that these workshops could not have been as professional as they were without Jackie's direct input. Jackie carried out all of the administration action by typing up all of my teaching notes, by preparing all of the certificates, by booking venues and by carrying out the administration tasks surrounding each delegate's booking, and so on. She did this with never a dissenting word. Again, I must record my sincere thanks to all of the wonderful support that Jackie gave to me during the days of my angel workshops. She is indeed an earth angel herself.

I really enjoyed running the workshops, and following one workshop, Bella and Chrystal came to visit me together. They told me that I would be expanding my angel workshops and that the workshops themselves would contain much more direct angel input. Many of the people that were now going to be led to the workshops needed to be taken to new levels in their own spiritual development. I felt very comfortable running the workshops that I had to date and equally I felt very comfortable at the thought of expanding the workshops, both in terms of frequency and in terms of the volume of people attending.

Expansion of Angel Workshops

I was really happy to expand the angel workshops in the way that the angels wanted. For example, rather than just running the three individual one-day workshops for beginner, intermediate and advanced level, I was now also running a two-day workshop. These were generally held over a weekend and these particular two-day workshops had the effect of generating even more energy on day two, following on from the previous day. This was also a microcosm of what happened at the angel therapy course in America; each day generated wonderful energy, but that energy was magnified considerably on the following day. It was almost a cumulative approach, so by holding a combined two-day workshop, this enabled the energies from day one to be magnified considerably on the following day of the workshop.

I also developed a different workshop model, in having a one-day intensive workshop that selected all of the key components from what hitherto had been three separate one-day workshops. All of the differing workshops that I presented, on behalf of the angels, were delivered to the people that were right to be there at that particular time. This enabled me to employ a menu-type approach for workshop attendees, so they could select the workshop or workshops that best suited their personal needs and development requirements. Obviously, the expansion of the angel workshops also gave the opportunity for much greater in-depth training and development for attendees on a wide variety of subjects. For example, three particular areas were specifically chosen to help develop all attendees at the workshops, irrespective of their previous experience in this field. These three areas were angel card readings, automatic writing and the four clairs.

To give a brief overview of these particular areas, I will list some of the key components.

Angel Card Readings

For angel card readings, I instructed individuals how to forge a better connection with their angels and how to relax their mental state and to let go of their ego-mind, which would allow their own higher mind to come to the fore and the angel card readings to flow more naturally. Once this state was achieved, then obviously the angels found it far easier to make contact with the angel card reader, which would allow true angelic readings to flow through.

Automatic Writing

The automatic writing training delivered a similar mindset to the workshop attendees, taking them into a meditation scenario where they became totally relaxed. They worked in pairs to carry out this particular exercise and the automatic writing would flow more naturally once the training had been given.

The Four Clairs

The four clairs are a vitally important piece in the jigsaw in being able to contact angels and indeed spirits in general. Each of the four clairs relates to a different spiritual gift. I will list these in no particular order of importance, as they are all important in their own right.

- Clairvoyance is the ability to see spirit.
- Clairaudience is the ability to hear spirit.
- Clairsensience is the ability to sense and feel spirit.
- Claircognisance is that deep, inner knowing you get, and can be supplemented by repetitive thoughts, which the angels give us.

Each of these four clairs can be developed and the workshops were also aimed at developing all four clairs at an appropriate pace for each of the workshop attendees.

It is absolutely vital for me to stress at this stage that this is the area where human beings need to be at their most discerning. All four clairs can indeed be increased and anybody on a spiritual path seeking to develop these should do so in a loving and safe environment, with a sympathetic and trusting teacher, to ensure that the teachings are of the highest good.

I carried out many angel workshops in the one-day intensive and two-day mode and again Archangel Michael and Archangel Ariel attended every single one. I greatly appreciate all of the protection Archangel Michael gave the workshop attendees and I throughout the running of the workshops, and I also am grateful to Archangel Ariel for attending. In fact, I see Archangel Ariel as the symbol, or emblem, of my angel workshops. Her presence was always valued and her input was also concise and of great clarity.

I will not go into the details of any of the specifics that happened at any of the angel workshops, as it would not be right to do so in this book, but needless to say the wonderful emotions and the energies that flowed throughout the workshops were a sight to behold. There were many times when tears were shed by workshop attendees and some of the things that happened and some of the angels that presented themselves were too miraculous to describe. Even those of a hardcore, doubting disposition could not have failed to have been touched by the energies and the angelic presence that was generated during these workshops. The angels never fail us, they never fail to attend when they need to, they never fail in their drive and determination to make contact with us human beings and they never fail in their sole purpose of being messengers from the divine source to us. If only we could all slow down just a little bit, if only we could all open our hearts to allow the angels in, then the world would be a much better place and our lives would be so greatly enriched.

A Family Tragedy

In the autumn of 2007, Jackie and I were delighted to hear from Kerry, our eldest daughter, that she was pregnant. Our youngest daughter, Hayley, had three healthy boys and Jackie and I love our three grandchildren greatly, so it was with great joy that Jackie and I heard of Kerry's news and we were delighted for both her and her husband, James. Jackie and I were not sure how long Kerry and James had been trying for a baby but you could just see the joy in their faces when they told us that Kerry was expecting. Kerry and James did the same as most new parents-to-be would do: they began to decorate the baby's bedroom in their house and purchased all of the essential things such as a cot, pushchair, pram, and so on.

While Jackie and I already had three grandsons, we really did not mind what the sex was of Kerry's baby; after all this was another grandchild that Jackie and I could love as much as our existing three grandsons, Thomas, Benjamin and William.

In the first few months of her pregnancy, poor Kerry was so, so sick. She suffered acute sickness throughout the first four months or so of the pregnancy, and no matter what anti-sickness tablets she was made to take by the GPs and hospital, the treatment had no effect. In fact, at one stage, Kerry was hospital-ised for a few days, as the sickness got so bad. Kerry was looking extremely ill and when she was hospitalised she was put on steroids as well as anti-sickness medication via a drip in an attempt to stop her acute sickness. Nothing seemed to work however. All tests on the baby were totally normal and this was a great relief to all of the family and no doubt to Kerry and James in particular.

After about twenty weeks or so, the sickness that Kerry was experiencing eased off a bit and she was not as bad as she had hitherto been. No doubt the steroids and anti-sickness medica-tion had helped somewhat, but she was still a shadow of her former self. She had almost lost her spark, which is no surprise when one considers the amount of weeks that she was being violently ill. Even though Kerry felt very ill most of the time during the pregnancy, she and James, and indeed the whole of the family, were greatly looking forward to the birth of their baby.

In early February 2008, Kerry had attended an aqua natal class for pregnant mothers. Kerry used to like attending the aqua natal class because it gave her a chance to speak to other mothers in the same position as herself, as well as an opportunity to undertake a limited form of physical exercise and also to receive the other benefits that aqua natal can bring. At the aqua natal class, however, Kerry was concerned that she had not felt the baby move for the last day or so and she told her midwife of this. The midwife arranged for Kerry to attend a hospital in Gosport called the War Memorial Hospital for a scan. The medical team at the War Memorial Hospital advised Kerry that the scan results were of significant concern to them and that Kerry needed to go to Winchester Maternity Hospital as a matter of some urgency. Kerry got hold of her husband James, and they duly drove to the hospital's maternity unit. I received a text from James relatively early in the evening, advising me that they were on the way to the maternity unit and that he feared the worst.

I immediately contacted Jackie and picked her up from work so that we could also go to the hospital and met Kerry and James there. As we walked into the hospital, Kerry and James were waiting in the reception and we could see by the look on their face that we were about to be advised of the most devastating news. Kerry's baby had died within her womb. Kerry had two further scans at the maternity unit and these scans did indeed confirm that the baby had died. As Kerry was now in excess of twenty-five weeks pregnant, the maternity staff advised her that she needed to give birth to the baby naturally. The thought of this at the time was terribly heart wrenching and I could tell from Kerry's face that she was not looking forward to having to go through this particular step, perhaps not at all surprisingly.

I specifically asked one of the medical team whether or not they would consider carrying out a caesarean if that is what Kerry wanted, but the medical team, in the circumstances that they faced, needed Kerry to give birth naturally. Both Kerry and James were obviously emotionally broken by what had happened to them, and indeed Jackie and I felt likewise, but obviously nobody could feel to the same depth that Kerry and James did.

Jackie and I also got in touch with Hayley, Kerry's sister, who over the next week or so would go on to provide the most wonderful support that a sister ever could in such distressing circumstances.

Kerry was given drugs to induce the birth of the baby and the baby, a boy, was duly born at 5.15 p.m. on 8 February 2008. There were some procedural things that needed to be carried out on that day also, and perhaps the most distressing of them was the completion of a death certificate, which was obviously dated with the same day as the birth.

Kerry and James were given a private room at the maternity unit and the staff at the unit were truly magnificent, giving as much support to Kerry and James as possible. Nothing could ease the distress that Kerry and James felt and nothing will ever take away the memory and the pain of that particular day. Kerry and James spent the evening and the night with their baby and they slept together in the bed with the baby between them. The emotions that were felt were truly indescribable. Kerry and James were visited by the hospital chaplain and a christening service was arranged, also to take place on the day of the baby's birth. The baby was duly christened on 8 February 2008. He was named Matthew Jeffrey Stephen Rudge.

The christening service was carried out by the Reverend Maria Hooper, who was kind, considerate and understanding through-out the christening service. Only the direct family attended the christening service, which was held in the room where Matthew had been born. Those attending were Kerry and James, Jackie and I, Hayley, and James's stepmother, Diana. One of the midwives from the hospital also attended, as obviously did Reverend Maria Hooper.

I think it is fair to say that the family had never been faced with such sadness. To see little Matthew lying in his crib or in Kerry's arms, so lifeless, was truly heartbreaking. He was a beautiful boy and I am sure he would have gone on to become a wonderful man. The loss that Kerry and James feel specifically, and the loss that the whole family feel generally, can never be replaced. We will always hold a candle in our hearts for beautiful baby Matthew.

Matthew was taken away from Kerry and James the following day by the hospital staff, who said they now needed to move on with the investigation into Matthew's death. Kerry had agreed for Matthew to be transferred to a specialist unit in London for a post-mortem to be undertaken. We were told that the results could take four to six weeks and that there was very little like-lihood of finding out an exact cause of death but Kerry and James felt that they needed to hold the post-mortem just to see if any answers could be given. The early advice that we were given turned out to be correct, as there were no specific causes of Matthew's passing. We will never know why Matthew passed; all we do know is that we all miss him terribly.

Matthew's funeral was held on 19 February 2008 at Portchester Crematorium in Hampshire. Kerry and James were obviously heartbroken at the funeral service itself, and while James tried to find that inner male strength to keep him going, he was suffering as much as Kerry, but he handled his loss in a different way. Kerry has always worn her heart on her sleeve and it was obvious to all who saw her at that time that she was indeed a broken figure. To this day, Kerry still suffers badly from the loss of Matthew and perhaps not surprisingly she will take this feeling to her grave, too. We all pray that time itself does ease the burden and the pain that Kerry feels, and we also pray that she and James can go on to have successful childbirths in the future, and while no other child could replace Matthew, Kerry and James could at least have another child or children as an outlet for their parental love.

From my own perspective, during this difficult time I often spoke with Bella, Chrystal and Amhiel, and indeed other angels that I saw, and became very cross with them. I know I was not right to feel this or to say some of the things I said to the angels, but Kerry's hurt and Kerry's pain was so great that I often almost screamed at the angels as to how they could let something so terrible happen. I clearly remember asking Chrystal on many occasions, and Bella also, that as the angels are so powerful, how they could let something so traumatic happen to somebody who had so much love to give to her baby.

Bella always told me that Matthew had gone to a place where his own spiritual development would be so vast and so great that he would always be an inspiration to Kerry. Matthew would always be a light that Kerry would be drawn to. Matthew would always be that twinkle that we see in the most beautiful of stars in the sky. I often took great comfort from some of the things that Bella said, but it still did not take away the exasperation that I felt.

Bella told me that it would be impossible for me to fully comprehend all of the reasons and all of the logic behind what had happened, and indeed what has happened in many world catastrophes, but Bella did say that things happen for a reason and that often, prior to birth, choices are made by us all that manifest here on earth in challenges that we feel that we could never face and never overcome.

The only solace I could give to Kerry and James is to pass on some specific words that Bella said to me. She said that Matthew is in a wonderful place; he is surrounded by love, he is surrounded by light, he does not feel the pain that we feel, that it is a burden that we have to carry here on earth, but we should receive strength from the knowledge that Matthew is truly happy.

I sincerely trust that these words will go some way to ease the suffering that Kerry and James have felt and are feeling to this day.

Falling off the Path

For many months after Matthew's passing, I tended to withdraw into myself in terms of angel contact. Jackie and I always tried to be as supportive as we could to Kerry and James through their difficult period, and as I mentioned previously, Hayley was also a fantastic support to them both. Hayley produced a book to commemorate Matthew's presence here on earth and it was a book that contained all sorts of mementos and all sorts of memories that Kerry and James will treasure for the rest of their lives. Hayley truly is a jewel in the crown, coming to the fore at times of family tragedy or family suffering. I did not intend to withdraw into myself, and to withdraw yet again from the angels, especially as I had promised them on many occasions that I would not step back from them any more, but it was just how I felt.

I could not say that Matthew's passing in any way shook my faith because I know what I know. I see angels and hear angels with such clarity that I know with every fibre in my being that they exist, so how could I ever say that my faith was shaken? All I can say is that I chose to step back from them once again, while I entered the spiral of decline that many humans do when faced with mental distress. I felt quite run down and low, and while this was nothing compared with how Kerry and James must have felt, from my own perspective it was yet another knock to add to the many things that I had faced over the years.

Bella was extremely prominent during this time and I used to get great comfort from chatting to her about a whole host of issues. Bella has an incredible knack of knowing exactly how I feel prior to arriving to see me. There are many occasions when she just sits there and talks to me about day-to-day things and all sorts of things that, looking back, could be seen as trivial in nature, but Bella and indeed all angels are happy to give comfort in whatever way is necessary. Sometimes she would talk to me specifically about things, things that were relevant to me at the time if she felt that would help, and there were other times when she would just generalise about a whole host of issues, without talking about me or referring to anything specific in my life at all. Bella is indeed a master at knowing what to say and when to say it.

I used to see Chrystal occasionally at this time as well, but Chrystal's visits were much fewer and farther between. Even Chrystal seemed to take a back seat when it came to nudging me back on to the path to carry on with my next steps in terms of spiritual development of either myself or others. I have always wondered how the angels spoke to each other and how they decided who would see me and when. I have asked this on occasion, but again it is one of those questions that the angels just smile at. They obviously just know which of them or which group of them should appear and when they should appear, and what they should say. What a wonderful gift that is and how wonderful it would be if us humans could only share that gift!

Another few months passed without any great changes happening in my life, and Bella's visits started to wind down simultaneously with Chrystal's visits increasing. It was almost as though they were passing a baton between them, one to the other. Bella's comforting visits had started to decrease in number and Chrystal's nudging and more proactive visits had started to increase. At the time, I had not noticed the way that this had taken place but, looking back, it is now obvious to me that I was being nudged to get back on to the spiritual path that I had chosen to step off. I think there are many times in the human life cycle when even the most devout spiritual followers step off the path for one particular reason or another. In my experience, generally we always get a calling to come back on to that path, and whether that timescale is a matter of weeks, months, years or even decades, at the appropriate time, that calling gets so strong and so loud that it is impossible to resist any further. Some people, however, go through whole lifetimes without that calling coming to the fore, but when it is appropriate, that calling will be so loud that it will be impossible to resist.

Climbing Back up the Ladder

After many conversations with Bella and Chrystal in particular, I began to feel the calling once again to get back on to a spiritual path. Over the preceding month or so, I had received many visitations from those of the angelic realms, not least from my trio of angels but also with other angels and light beings. It was during one such visitation that the idea of writing a book was first mentioned to me.

I had never once given previous thought to writing a book and I certainly could never see myself having the patience to do so. On one particular morning, however, I received a visitation from an angel who was dressed in what seemed like pure gold and also had a golden aura. This particular angel had an extremely strong presence and I was almost knocked off my feet when the angel first appeared.

The angel was certainly of feminine form and initially she seemed to have an Egyptian look about her. It looked as though she had gold bracelets or bangles going up her arm and also had a stunning golden necklace on. Her eyes were much darker than other angels I had previously seen and the outline of the eye was very dark and clearly marked. The eyes themselves also seemed very dark, almost black in colour, and the angel had the most piercing of looks. I could clearly see that this being had angelic wings, although these were rather faded in comparison to the rest of her body and the aura that I could clearly see.

She spoke only briefly but what she did say was to be of some importance later on in my life. She said that my angel workshops were delivering some excellent results and I was passing on the angelic messages that I was given and this pleased the angels greatly. She continued by saying, however, that there were many other messages that I needed to pass on and that many of these were not being spoken of during the angel workshops. She said that I had been concentrating on delivering the same sort of training that I had had from Doreen Virtue and some of the other direct training that I had received from the angels, and while this was commendable, there were many other forms of training that I had previously received from the angels, either while I was awake or in my sleep state, that the angels wanted me to pass on.

She said that these messages were lying deep within me and I needed to open up in order to fully bring these messages back to the surface, so that I could do justice in passing them on during my teachings. I said that I had never deliberately or knowingly held on to anything that I had been asked to pass on and I was certainly not aware of any deep-lying messages within me that I needed to pass on. She smiled at this point and said to me that these messages would be brought to the surface very soon and I would need to pass these on, or act in accordance with the message, at the appropriate time. I promised the angel that I would do just that.

She then went on to say that I would be writing a series of books that would pass on some of the important messages that the angels had. I in turn smiled at this and thought to myself that I could never see myself writing a book or becoming an author. Instantaneously, the angel knew my thoughts and said that I would indeed be writing a series of books. I took that comment at face value and just nodded in approval. With that the angel vanished. She went as quickly as she had arrived and I have never seen her again.

I began to feel much more connected again, which for me is an incredibly important feeling to have and is almost part of my very life force. When I next saw Bella, I asked her who the angel was that had visited me and talked about writing a book and had the most beautiful of golden auras. Bella said this particular angel was from a realm that I previously had not had much contact with, but the angel from this particular realm had chosen to make contact with me on that particular occasion. I said to Bella that I had certainly felt a difference in pressure and presence during this particular angel visitation, and while knowing that there was a difference between her energy and most other angel energies that I had encountered, I was at a loss to explain the difference.

Bella asked me to pay particular attention to my thoughts. She said that I had started to become a little too focused on only picking up what the angels had said to me when they were speaking to me. She said that the angels' preferred method of communication remained through thought. She said many in the human race only ever picked up anything an angel or spirit said if they did in fact hear it, but on the grounds that most people do not see or hear their angels, the angels have to choose a different method of communication. Two of their preferred methods are through feelings and thought and this is where clairsentience and claircognisance comes in.

With many people being clairsentient in their primary clair – in other words, clairsentience is the strongest of their clair abilities – it is important to pay particular attention to any feelings or emotions that you have. For example, if you feel tearful for no reason and these are tears of joy, it could well be a sign that your guardian angel is close to you. Equally, if you have recurring thoughts or recurring ideas, this could well be your guardian angel trying to communicate with you in the method where you can best receive their message. It is particularly important to pay attention to your recurring thoughts and your recurring ideas, as these could well be your guardian angel passing on a vitally important piece of information to you.

I know of many people who have angelic experiences in their thought forms but choose to ignore them and choose to listen to their ego-mind and head-mind and make decisions that are totally the opposite of what the angelic thought was trying to get across. So during the workshops that I held, I asked attendees to pay particular attention to their recurring thoughts and their recurring ideas, for within them could be an acorn of some wonderful experience that could grow into the equivalent of a majestic oak tree.

I often feel that the most successful entrepreneurs pick up thoughts from their angels and develop those thoughts and come up with some innovation that makes them truly famous, or truly rich, without them ever realising that the original thought came from their guardian angel.

While I had not planned to run any further angel workshops at this time in my life, I did run a couple of ad hoc workshops, which went very well indeed. These were workshops that I had not specifically planned but that people had asked for, and I duly ran them when the need arose.

At this stage, I was paying more attention to my circle work. I was beginning to attend a particular circle that went into spiritual matters in a very deep way indeed. It was during one particular circle that it was made known to me what some of my next steps would be on my spiritual path. There were four people at this particular circle and the circle leader had just wrapped up the circle when I could clearly hear a voice saying to me that there was an important next step I needed to take. I have no idea where the voice came from and I certainly could not see anybody else in the room of a spiritual nature at that time. The circle itself duly ended, and I had a cup of tea and a couple of chocolate biscuits along with the other circle members and bade them farewell as I began to go to the car to make my way home.

While driving home, I could hear a voice in the back of the car, asking me to pull over at an appropriate time. This was not the first time that I had heard a voice in the back of the car but on this particular night I was a little reluctant to pull over so I just chose to drive all the way home and parked up outside of my house. With that, I turned round to look in the back seat of the car and there materialising in front of my very eyes was an incredible being of great strength. I am not sure whether he was from the angelic realms but he certainly had an extremely strong presence about him. I could not see any angel wings or suchlike and he was totally of human form, but I knew that he was from a realm of the higher levels. The gentleman spoke very clearly to me. He had a beard and he looked relatively thin and it was hard to make out any height with him sitting in the back seat of the car but I would imagine he was about five foot ten inches tall. He had long wavy hair, which matched the colour of his beard, which was dark brown. It was difficult to see clearly because it was night-time and there were no external lights present, although it was a moonlit night, which did give some clarity to the gentleman in question.

He spoke very clearly and he said to me that I had carried out some good work at the circle that I had been attending and that spirits were readying my energy levels for some vitally important work that they wanted me to carry out. I listened intently as the gentleman said that the work would entail spirit rescue. I had certainly carried out some element of spirit rescue in the circles that I had been attending, but I had not carried it out to the level that this gentleman was now alluding to. I said, however, that I would be delighted to do this and I asked for guidance on what needed to be done. I was told that spirit would do all in its power to get me ready for the work that I needed to undertake. There would be a whole range of things that I would be shown and a whole range of things that I would be taught, all of which would culminate in getting me fully ready for the spirit rescue work that spirit wanted me to undertake.

Having carried out some spirit rescue work already, I was delighted to be asked to take this on even further and to deal with even more troubled spirits than had hitherto been the case.

With that, the gentleman vanished and everything returned to normal in terms of energy within the car.

A few days later, Chrystal appeared at a time when I was not expecting any angel visitation at all. I had decided that I was indeed delighted to be chosen to undertake some further spirit rescue work, but on this occasion I went with what the angels had previously told me: I totally surrendered and let go any thought or any planning on my part to undertake this spirit rescue work. I just sat back and waited for something to happen.

When Chrystal appeared, I could sense that she was keen to say something to me, as her whole demeanour seemed different to what is normally the case with Chrystal. While she is always generally nudging me to do something else or to move on into a new chapter of my life, on this occasion she seemed even more forthright in her demeanour. She said that over the preceding few months, I had noticed and seen many spirits but generally had not engaged them in any form of communication, or indeed tried to communicate with them to see if they needed any assistance or help. She said she could understand this, having suffered the family tragedy that we had all encountered. She said on this occasion, however, that while I was not in any position to help in the case of poor Matthew, I was in a position to readily assist and help all forms and manner of spirit in the rescue work that I needed to undertake.

Chrystal asked me not to pass up the opportunity to help these spirits. She said that from an emotional perspective, a spirit in need of rescue suffers as a human being would suffer in terms of the emotion that is attached to whatever their particular problem or issue was. She said that the spirits were asking a lot of me, and expecting a lot of me, and I was not to take on this task lightly. She said that many spirits would come to me, as they would see the light that I had within me and around me, and they would be attracted to that, as they would see the light that they themselves were seeking.

Chrystal continued by saying that many spirits that are in need of rescue, as I had been told previously, have no idea that they have passed from this life to the spirit world, and that those individuals in particular are in need of desperate help in order to pass them over to the light for their own spiritual progression. She also said that many spirits that are earthbound choose to be so but that they themselves also need help and assistance to pass over to the light. Chrystal said that the human emotions that one has while alive remain with us initially when we pass and that some of those emotions, especially those of anger and hatred, need to be cleansed in order to ensure that the spirit passes over seamlessly and painlessly to the light. I was well aware of the points that Chrystal was making, having already carried out some limited form of spirit rescue work, and I said that I would assist in any way that I could.

I acknowledged to Chrystal that I had once again fallen off of the spiritual path due to the pressures and stresses that being a human can bring, but that I – and I knew this within every fibre of my being – was now ready to climb back up the spiritual ladder. Even though on many occasions I have fallen off of the spiritual path, or decided to step off of the spiritual path, I always have that calling, whether that be a matter of weeks or months later, and I am always delighted to go back to the warm embrace of spirit and angels.

Chrystal asked me to engage some of the spirits that I would be seeing in the near future, to actually undertake a dialogue with them and to ask them specifically if they were in need of help or assistance and to offer my service to assist them. She said that initially some spirits may cold-shoulder me once they realised what my intentions were, especially those spirits that still held fear or anger and for whatever reason did not feel ready to pass to the light. I said to Chrystal that I would certainly now start to take up the baton in this area and engage any spirits that I did see, especially those I felt I could help. The thought of a spirit being stranded on the earth plane and not moving forward into the light for their own spiritual progression is truly horrendous. All spirits should return to the light in order to undertake the next steps that are right for them at soul level. Spirit had told me that I was ready to undertake this spirit rescue work, the angels had told me that I was ready to undertake this spirit rescue work and within my heart I also knew that I was ready to undertake this work.

I was shortly to be exposed to the many spirits that did indeed need rescue and I was faced with many challenges that I needed to overcome in order to assist certain spirits. Little did I realise just how much I would need the assistance of angels to undertake this work. I initially thought that I could do most of the work single-handedly. How wrong I was. Without the direct intervention and support of the angels, none of what followed could have been possible.

Spirit Rescue

Following on from my discussions with Chrystal regarding the next steps for my spirit rescue work, little did I realise just how many spirits were indeed earthbound for one reason or another and that need rescue. There are those spirits that refuse to accept that they have passed over. There are spirits that are held back on earth because of an emotional attachment, there are spirits that are refusing to go to the light for their own reasons and there are spirits who stay as a result of their own anger and fear.

Of course, there are many other reasons why spirits become earthbound, and in their own right they are all in need of some assistance. I know of many mediums who hold spirit rescue circles and do individual spirit rescue work and these mediums do an absolutely wonderful job in the work that they undertake. They are working for the light and on behalf of the light and that is truly commendable.

While I had carried out some spirit rescue work myself, being a member of a spirit rescue circle, and indeed some of the other mediumship activity I undertook, I thought I would try something a little more formal, trying to set aside specific time in order to carry out the work that Chrystal had asked me to undertake. With that in mind, on one particular day, I decided to sit alone in my house while Jackie was at work, go into a meditative state and actually ask the angels to guide towards me any spirits that needed rescue. I am not sure how the angels do this, and indeed how they channel spirits to somebody like myself when I formally sit to undertake spirit rescue work, but it must have been only a matter of minutes before a spirit appeared standing directly in front of me.

This particular spirit was a girl in her teens (I would estimate her age to be about eighteen) and she spoke very eloquently and slowly. The thing that I immediately noticed was the American accent that she had. She told me that her name was Mary and that she did indeed live in America. I suppose from a spirit perspective, distance on earth is nothing as spirits can travel just by thought and go from point A to point B in milliseconds, or to be more precise, instantaneously.

I asked Mary if she knew where she was and why she chose to visit me. I could tell that she was a little bit confused but she said that she had been guided to me so that I could help her. After a few more minutes of general chat, I asked Mary if she knew that she had actually passed over. I could tell in Mary's eyes and by her reaction that she knew she had indeed died, but she seemed reluctant to accept this. She told me about her family circumstances and of her death, which was rather horrific. I felt great empathy for Mary; she was obviously concerned over her relatives that would be left on earth and were indeed mourning her loss. I said to Mary that I would ask the angels to go to Mary's family and to surround them with love and light to help their grieving process and to enable them to move on in whatever way was best for them. I told Mary that her moving over to the light herself would in no way detract from her family still thinking of her, from Mary thinking of them, or from them still to have contact, even if that was only by thoughts of remembrance.

Mary gave me the impression that she was quite drained and tired and I asked her whether she would be willing now to pass over to the light. She asked me what that entailed and how that would be achieved. I told Mary that I would ask the angels to appear in the room with us both at that time, and that I would ask one of the angels to hold Mary's hand and to just gently move towards the light that would be encircling her. I could tell by Mary's reaction that she was indeed ready. With that, I asked the angels to come to Mary and to guide her towards the light. Two angels appeared, standing together in the far corner of the room. They did not approach either Mary or me directly at all; they just stood there, holding out one hand towards her.

Mary looked at me and I looked at Mary. She looked at me in such a way that she was asking me a question. I just smiled at Mary and nodded. She smiled back and took a few paces towards the angels. Both angels, as I said, had their hands held out towards her and she reached out with both of her hands to touch the hands of the angels. Just before she took another step forward, she turned to look at me and smiled. I once again smiled back and Mary took another pace towards the angels and, with that, they all vanished.

I then saw something that I had not seen before during spirit rescue. Just as Mary and the two angels vanished, the corner of the room where this took place was surrounded in sparkling light. If you can imagine the sparks that come off of a sparkler at fireworks parties, then that is what the corner of the room was shrouded in, thousands of little sparkles of light, flickering in and out of focus. This must have only lasted for a couple of seconds, but it was a wonderful sight to behold.

I sat for a few more moments like that but no other spirit appeared, so I decided to break the formality of that particular session and to stretch and come out of the meditation session that I was in. All of this was conducted with my eyes wide open and when I call it a meditation session, I mean it was almost an altered state of consciousness. It is a more relaxed, calm feeling about the mind and body, which in turn raises the vibration of the human being to allow the spirit world to make contact with us.

I thought of Mary for many days after and while I have never had any feedback specifically about her, I know that she is in the best place for her now and I truly hope that her family are coming to terms with the loss that they must have felt and will feel to this day.

As well as what I call the formal session of that particular spirit rescue, I also later saw other spirits that were in need of rescue, without any specific trying on my part. One night a few weeks later, I was awoken during the night by a soft voice in the corner of my room. I looked up and there was a lady standing there. This lady had medium-length black hair and she was dressed in quite an old-fashioned outfit.

She was a charming lady and we must have chatted for a good few minutes. She told me some things about herself and then asked me whether I would paint a picture of her. I had to laugh at that because I have never been able to draw or paint and the thought of being able to paint a picture of this lady definitely brought a smile to my face. I told her that I could not paint or draw but that I would bear that in mind and if there was ever an occasion where I could paint a picture of this lady, then I would definitely do so. She looked at me in a knowing way, almost as if she knew that I would indeed paint a picture of her, but as of this moment in time, I have still not done that. I think that I would need the hand of spirit to guide my hand, when I attempted this!

Occasionally I also saw spirits standing by the roadside or just walking about in town centres, and it was always very difficult to ascertain whether I should engage these spirits or whether I should just acknowledge them. Either way, Chrystal had encouraged me to start to engage spirits on a much more frequent basis and to actually ask whether they needed any help from me. Sometimes I asked this by thought alone and there were some occasions when I got no response at all from the particular spirit. I have latterly found out from Chrystal, and indeed another angel, that some of these spirits respond in a much more positive way if I actually speak to them out loud so they can speak back. I can only assume that is something to do with the vibration of the voice that helps the spirit hear what is being said, or perhaps they are not evolved enough to hold a conversation by thought alone. Whatever the reason, I now, on a much more frequent basis, talk to the spirits as I would talk to anybody else. One has to be careful here, however, and I always make sure that I don't speak out loud to any spirit if I am in a public place!

Occasionally I still hold what I called earlier a formal spirit rescue session, just as I did when Mary was led to me, but on a much more frequent basis I just engage the spirits that I see whenever I am in a position to do so. There are of course many spirits that I do see where I cannot engage them for one reason or another, but if ever I am in a position to engage them, I always try to do so.

When I next saw Chrystal, I asked her whether or not there was anything else I needed to do in the way that I was approaching the spirit rescue work. Having now committed myself to carrying out this work, I wanted to ensure that I was doing it properly. Chrystal said that she felt that it was important that she describe to me a little bit of the process so that I could better understand what happened when the spirit actually passed from this world to the other. She also said that it was important that I asked the relevant guides or angels to assist me on every occasion when the actual passing of the spirit was taking place. There had been some occasions where I passed spirit myself. Chrystal said it was very important that I always asked for the angels to assist in the actual passing of the spirit. She said to me that on some occasions the spirit that actually passes over is in a very confused state and is full of fear, as they do not know what is going to happen to them. Depending on the 'condition' of the spirit, then that would decide where the spirit will first pass when it crosses the veil into the world of spirit. For example, some truly advanced spirits will probably go straight through to a higher level in the spirit world, whereas those in a state of fear are more likely to go into a lower level of the spirit world, one where they will need a period of convalescence before moving on.

Chrystal said that I did not need to ask for any particular angels to assist in passing spirits over and I could just use the collective term 'angels' in calling for them to assist the spirit passing. Certainly under normal events my trio of angles would not be involved in the actual passing of spirits and in the majority of cases, I see one of the two angels that assisted Mary, or different angels altogether. Some of these could of course be the guardian angel of the person themselves. The assistance of angels is greatly appreciated in performing spirit rescue work and that is particularly true for spirits that, for whatever reason, do not voluntarily wish to leave the earth plane. Obviously spirits are never dragged screaming, so to speak, into the spirit world; I have only ever witnessed spirits going voluntarily, with angels gently coaxing them to follow them into the light.

Chrystal said that I also needed to have a better appreciation of what life was like on the other side of the veil, as she said that many of the spirits that I will assist in passing will almost certainly benefit from an explanation about what awaits them. From a general perspective, whereas the earth plane is high tempo, high stress and fast forward in its approach and generally pressured, the spirit world is the total opposite in that it is a world of calmness, relaxation and one of great knowledge and learning opportunities. Chrystal said that, later on, the angels would give me a far greater appreciation of life beyond the veil. I had many questions to ask Chrystal regarding what happens to individual spirits when they first pass, but Chrystal said that more of that would be explained later.

Before departing on this particular occasion, she said to me that it may be worth me understanding a little bit about what happens to the human body at the moment of death. She said that generally the more gentle and serene it is when a human dies on earth, the greater the likelihood that the spirit would pass gently into the spirit world; conversely, therefore, the opposite is also true, on occasions. A more traumatic death on earth can result in a 'bumpy landing' in the spirit world. On these occasions, of course, a period of convalescence will generally be provided to that spirit in order to assist the transition.

Chrystal said that on the vast majority of occasions when a human being dies, they lapse into a gentle sleep. The spirit would then gently rise above the physical body, although at that stage it is still attached to the body by means of a bright silver cord; this is what some people refer to as the lifeline. This is the moment when those that are involved in spirit rescue from the spirit world themselves, or indeed angels, often arrive at the location of the deceased person. The bright silver cord, the lifeline, is then detached from the physical body. On occasions at this stage, the physical body would twitch as the lifeline itself detaches. This silver cord then retracts into spirit form and disappears totally, along with the spirit itself. This is the true moment of death. While on earth that is indeed the most traumatic time for the grieving relatives and loved ones left behind, this is the moment that the spirit crosses the veil and is actually fully alive and present. It is at this stage that the physical body is indeed just that: it was a vehicle, a physical body nonetheless, but a vehicle for the spirit. An overcoat if you like.

I have been involved in literally hundreds of spirit rescues since that day, and it is a great honour and a privilege to carry out this work. Obviously the vast majority of spirits just pass naturally and safely to the other side, and it is only the ones that become earthbound that are in need of spirit rescue and me and people like me try to assist in whatever way we can. The greatest role, however, is the one that is performed by the angels themselves and those of the spirit world who visit our world in order to help with the passing of those recently deceased.

I have come across many forms of spirit that have happily availed themselves of spirit rescue and equally I have come across a certain number of spirits that flatly refuse to cross over to the other side, and for those that have remained and chosen not to pass over, I truly hope that one day the angels can guide them to the light, for it is there that they will find true peace, true harmony and pure love.

Meeting the Archangels

One night towards the end of 2008, I was awoken by Chrystal, who said to me that it was important that I listened intently to what she had to say, as I was going to be given information concerning archangels that would be of great use to some individuals that I would be encountering in my later life.

Having conducted many angel workshops, I was well aware of many archangels and certainly the fifteen main archangels that I had been working with. I had not seen all of the fifteen archangels that I had been working with at the workshops, but I knew of most of their presences when they did assist in the workshops themselves, or in the follow-up activities. The archangels that I had seen on many occasions and had great knowledge of were the archangels Ariel, Gabriel, Jophiel, Michael and Raphael.

Chrystal asked me to close my eyes and relax, as she would be taking me on a journey. With that, I felt her hand touching my forehead and instantaneously Chrystal and I were in a very large room with bench-like seats all around the outside, and some more significant seats in the middle of the room. By significant, I mean they were almost of a throne-like stature. There must have been up to thirty of these seats, formed into a semicircle. Chrystal said nothing but she led me by the hand to stand about five feet away from the beginning of the semicircle of seats.

At that precise moment, angels appeared in every seat simultaneously. They were much larger than the angels I generally see on earth, and indeed much larger than many of the archangels that I had seen previously. Their presence was very powerful and I must admit that I felt rather in awe to be standing there before them. I looked at Chrystal and she looked at me in a way that just said I needed to say nothing. That may seem hard to describe but that is exactly the feeling that I had. I needed to say nothing; I just needed to be in the presence of these beings. With that, I heard some music but I could not tell where it was coming from. It seemed to be coming from before me, above me, behind me, to the side of me and was just all around and within me. It was the most beautiful of music, just like the song of a thousand birds singing at once in the most beautiful, synchronistic way.

I later found out that this was the music of the celestial choir and these beings that were sitting on the seats in front of me were very advanced celestial beings. I am sure they must have been archangels, although I do not know the names of these celestial beings. With that, one of the archangels spoke. He had a very authoritative voice. He spoke in words that I did not know; the language was one that I had not heard before but I was listening intently as he spoke. He raised one of his hands and a beam of light came out of the hand and engulfed the whole room. I was never asked to work these excessively long hours by my employer – far from it. Again, I said nothing but could feel the immense power that was in the room.

At this stage, I was totally unaware whether Chrystal was still standing to the side of me; I was just looking around at the light and feeling the warmth that it emitted. I remember feeling at the time how wonderful this was, then the light itself vanished, as did the celestial beings that were sitting in the seats. I looked round and there was just Chrystal and I left in the room.

I asked Chrystal who these celestial beings were and whether they were indeed archangels. She smiled and nodded, which I took as an affirmation that these were indeed archangels. Chrystal said nothing but again she led me by the hand through a door that was to the side of the room in which we had been standing, and the sight that I was met with was truly staggering.

If you can imagine the most beautiful garden that you could ever envisage in your mind's eye, the most beautiful flowers, the most beautiful colours and the most beautiful smells of the garden, and then if you could magnify that by a factor of a thousand, then perhaps you would be getting close to the garden that Chrystal and I were now standing in. This truly was an awesome sight.

Chrystal said that this was a garden of the angels and that she would soon be leaving me there for a period of time so that I could walk around the garden and communicate more directly with the archangels that I had previously worked with. I remember being engulfed in a feeling of pure joy at the very thought of this. Without any fear or trepidation, I started to walk around the gardens, which seemed to go on indefinitely, while Chrystal walked in the opposite direction, back into the building that we had just left.

I was standing next to some particularly beautiful flowers, which were pink in colour, and I was looking at them in a way that I have never ever looked at earthly flowers. It was as though they had a living essence of their own. They almost seemed to be pulsating and the sheer beauty of these flowers was a sight to behold. At that moment, I suddenly noticed that not only were the flowers pink but the whole area that I was standing in seemed to be bathed in a pink colour.

I was then shown a vision in my third eye of a lioness. I knew exactly what this meant. I turned round and there standing behind me was Archangel Ariel. She is one of the most beautiful angels you could ever see. She exudes bravery and courage; she is indeed an archangel of immense power. Archangel Ariel told me that she worked very closely with the elemental kingdom and that she loved going into this garden, the garden of angels, as it was a place of great wonder. I spoke to Archangel Ariel for some time regarding the elementals that I had encountered on earth and she gave some useful advice about how to reinforce my connection with elementals and how to use them better than hitherto I had done. Archangel Ariel said to me that I needed to walk further around the garden in order to meet some of the other archangels that were waiting to see me. I duly did this without a moment's hesitation.

The next archangel I saw was an archangel called Metatron. This particular archangel has immense power. I could not get too close to him as I felt I would be knocked off of my feet by the strength of his vibration. Archangel Metatron was surrounded by a violet aura. I did not speak to him as such, but I knew that one of his main aims was to assist in the development of children. Standing to the right of Archangel Metatron was Archangel Michael, an archangel that I have seen on many occasions. Once again his aura colour was a purple shade and I have always seen

Archangel Michael as an archangel of protection.

On this particular occasion, however, he did say something strange to me, or something that I thought was strange at the time. He said to me that he was trying to provide me with a backbone to live my truth. I did not analyse that at all at the time, but looking back now, I thought to myself how strange that I had previously fractured my spine in the physical form and here was Archangel Michael saying to me that he was providing me with a backbone to live my truth.

I was a bit put back by this because I really felt that I was doing quite well in trying to live my truth, but Archangel Michael told me that I was still doing a lot of my spirit work undercover, so to speak, and I should be proud of myself for the work that I was doing on behalf of the angels, just as the angels themselves were proud of me. I remember feeling that, while in the spirit world it was so easy to speak one's truth and to live one's truth, on earth with all of the conflicting demands and all of the conflicting thoughts and beliefs that other humans have, how difficult indeed it is to live one's truth. One day, perhaps the whole human race can indeed live in truth. The truth of the light within, the light that is within us all.

I noticed Archangel Raphael standing a bit further away from Michael and Metatron and he was surrounded by the colour green, which seemed to blend in so well with the natural colours of the garden. Archangel Raphael, who has incredible and fantastic healing ability, had the most serene look on this particular occasion. I did not speak to him directly but I was greatly privileged to see him put his hands up while I was standing near him and I could feel his healing aura surround me just as much as it was surrounding him. This made me feel very calm and at peace with myself and all that was around me. There were some other archangels that I spoke to and had brief encounters with during that particular visit but I did not find out their names, and rather surprisingly for me, I did not even ask their names, so I can safely say my analytical mind was indeed put to bed!

I have no idea how long I was in the garden for, but it seemed to be for ages. I was suddenly aware that Chrystal was standing over in one corner of the garden and I started to make my way to her. I was hoping that Chrystal would say that we could stay even longer in the garden and explore some of the other wonderful sights that were befalling me but Chrystal said that it was now time to return. I walked alongside Chrystal as she walked back into the buildings that we had come from. I said nothing and she said nothing.

Once we were back in the room with the half-circle of chairs, she turned and faced me and held out both her hands. I reached out to hold Chrystal's hand and with that we were suddenly back in my bedroom. Chrystal looked at me lovingly. On this particular occasion, her energy was one of total tranquillity; she was not pushing me or nudging me to do anything. Her energy was much more like that of Bella, a comforting, supporting energy. I looked at Chrystal and without even saying a word, she could tell that I was truly grateful for where she had just led me. Chrystal left and I took a few paces back to get back into the bed.

I sat on the bed rather than lying down but I just could not get back to sleep at all, so I decided to go down and make myself a cup of tea and just sit for a period in silence, thinking about the wonders that I had just witnessed. I have never returned to the garden of the angels but I hope to revisit it one day when I cross over into the spirit world. It is a place of sheer beauty, sheer tranquillity, sheer serenity and sheer love. While the angels themselves are always here to help us human beings, and our guardian angels in particular are there to assist us as a messenger from God, the archangels are also there to assist us.

As I have mentioned previously, most archangels, while leading a team of angels themselves, also specialise in being what I would describe as a specialist in one particular area. If you, while reading this book, ever feel that you need an archangel to assist you, then it would be their pleasure to do so. I will list the fifteen main archangels now and this could help the reader in calling upon a particular archangel for something that they face at that particular time.

Table 1: The Main Archangels

Name	Meaning	Function	Aura Colour
Ariel	Lioness of God	Animals/bravery/courage. Oversees the elemental kingdom. Animal healer	Pale pink
Azrael	Who God helps	Counselling. Escort upon passing over	Vanilla cream
Chamuel	He who sees God	Love	Pink
Gabriel	God is my strength	Guidance: works with mothers and children and is the messenger angel for communication	White/ copper
Haniel	Grace of God	Provides grace and poise	Bluish white
Jeremiel	Mercy of God	Encourages life reviews and motivates us to devote time to acts of service	Purple
Jophiel	Beauty of God	Illumination and encourages outdoor lifestyle	Yellow
Metatron	Angel of the presence	Very powerful and develops children	Violet
Michael	He who is as God	Protection, and assists psychic children	Purple
Raguel	Friend of God	To act in a fair and just way. Is the champion of underdogs	Pale blue
Raphael	Whom God heals	Healing	Emerald green
Raziel	Secret of God	Turns ideas into gold	Rainbow
Sandalphon	Brother	Music and prayer	Turquoise
Uriel	The light of God	Peace, divine inspiration	Red/purple
Zadkiel	Righteousness of God	Joy, forgiveness and compassion	Violet

I was continuing with my spirit rescue work and on one particular day I was sitting on a bench in a park in Southsea in Portsmouth when I suddenly became aware of a spirit sitting next to me. The spirit was that of an elderly gentleman and initially I thought that the spirit was still in the human body as the clarity with which I saw him was very pronounced. I knew fairly quickly, however, that it was indeed a spirit when the gentleman said to me that he had come to me because he saw my light.

I asked him what he meant by that and he said that he was stepping out of a place of darkness and he was attracted to the light that I was showing. This is obviously similar to moths being attracted to the light at night. He said that he was trying to find the light, but that he couldn't leave the place that he was in. He did not go into a great deal of detail but I could tell that he was a tortured soul. Perhaps he had done something on earth that he truly regretted and the act that he had carried out perhaps had been so extreme that it filled him full of fear and horror. This in itself would manifest and magnify the darkness around him.

I told him that it did not need to be this way and that he could move to the light any time that he wanted. All he needed to do was to truly let go of his past, to hold out his hand and to say that he wanted to move on into the light. He said that he had tried to do exactly this on many occasions but that he always returned to the same dark place. I felt truly saddened to hear this.

Here was a spirit who was genuinely remorseful for whatever acts he had undertaken on earth, and he was trying to move to the light, but for whatever reason it was not happening for him.

This was the very first occasion that I called upon an archangel in particular to help me with the passing over of a spirit. Generally I just do exactly what Chrystal had said: ask the angels to help with the passing and allow them to decide what angels come through to help a spirit pass over. On this particular occasion, however, I just felt inclined, or indeed led, to call upon Archangel Azrael to help with this particular passing over.

As the gentleman was talking to me, I could tell his aura was very grey; he looked rather grey himself and certainly his aura was grey. In fact, while I was talking to him, the whole energy around him felt cold and it was like the feeling you would experience if you went into a damp cellar. After a few moments, I could tell that standing behind this gentleman was indeed an angel that was going to help me with the passing over. The light around the angel was a cream colour and at that moment I knew that Archangel Azrael had indeed arrived to help with the passing over.

I spoke to the gentleman and I asked him if he could see anything standing behind him. He turned to look and he said all he could see was a lighter colour. It was only at this stage that I realised everything that this gentleman was seeing was shrouded in darkness, and while he was attracted to the light that he initially said was around me, he still saw me through eyes that were coming out of the darkness so he really could not see any bright light at all. He was in an area that I would call the wilderness.

At that very moment, Archangel Azrael walked up closer to the gentleman and placed both of his hands on his shoulders. The gentleman just closed his eyes and whereas normally I see the angels guide the spirit in one particular direction and then they just walk into the light, on this occasion Archangel Azrael and the gentleman just faded away and I was suddenly just sitting on the park bench alone. I have absolutely no doubt that the gentleman was truly led over to the other side and Archangel Azrael and his supporting angels will have helped this gentleman pass to the light.

While I feel greatly encouraged to know that this gentleman is suffering no longer, I felt that he would spend a great deal of time in a period of convalescence before he could really move on into the next phase of his spiritual journey. He had obviously been through so much since his death and it is a great relief to me to know that he is now in the care of angels.

On a normal day-to-day basis, I generally just see one or two, or all three, of my trio of angels and a mixture of other angels that come and go depending on the situation that is around me at that particular time. I occasionally see an archangel in some form or another but generally this is very rarely on an unsolicited basis. On the vast majority of occasions, the only time I see an archangel or archangels is if I summon them or ask for their help for any particular reason. The archangels are just like the angels; they never let you down and they will also assist in any way they can.

Life Beyond the Veil

It took until early 2009 before Chrystal's conversation regarding being shown life beyond the veil actually came to fruition. It was in February of that year that the trio of angels appeared before me. I could tell by the three angels' energy that this was no normal meeting. They had not decided to arrive just for a general chat. I could sense that they had a real purpose to their visit and that something quite important was shortly to follow. Chrystal asked me if I recalled what she mentioned regarding being shown more details of what life is actually like in the spirit world. I said to Chrystal that certainly I remembered the conversation and that I was indeed looking forward to being shown this.

Chrystal said that that time had now come. She asked me to take a seat and make myself comfortable, and as we were in the lounge at the time, I sat in one of the two armchairs that we have and just sat back, waiting for the angels to tell me what to do next. Chrystal said that I needed to close my eyes, to block everything out of my mind and to hear no external noise other than her voice. Chrystal said that we would shortly be joined by another angel and this angel would provide me with the information that I needed to have a better understanding of the world beyond.

With that, I felt the presence of another angel in the room but I kept my eyes closed, as I was asked to do. This angel had a male presence but spoke in soft tones. He said that initially he wanted to tell me something prior to him showing me information of life in the spirit world.

He said, 'Robert, there are no judges when you pass over to the other side. There is not a great judge, there is not a chair of judges, there is not a board of judges; there are no judges to anything any human being has ever done on earth.'

He said there is something far more powerful than that; he said every human being will judge for themselves what they have done and why they did what they did. He said when a human passes to the spirit world, the spirit becomes extremely critical of itself and everything that happened on earth. He said that the spirit will sit with the angels of powers, who will help it and guide it during its own review of its particular life. He said that there is therefore no such thing as Judgement Day, there is no such thing as being sent to a place for offenders, there is no great judge and jury; there never has been and there never will be. Each spirit, each soul, will review its own life and make whatever commitments are necessary in order to try to put right any wrongdoings.

This can take many forms. It can be in the form of reincarnation to earth itself or to take whatever appropriate steps are necessary in the spirit world to make amends for those wrongdoings. The angel said to me that it was important for mankind to know this and he then said he would be taking me on a journey to view some of the areas in the spirit world that would stand me in good stead for the spirit rescue work that I was undertaking and would continue to undertake.

I felt myself being transported somehow. I was aware of my physical body sitting in the armchair but equally I was aware of my spirit form being transported. My eyes were still closed but I could sense that there were lights all around me. It was as though I was on an express train going through a kaleidoscope of colours.

After a short moment, and this certainly felt rather abrupt, I was aware of standing in a field. I was with an angel. He had no wings and he was of human form, but I knew he was an angel. It became clear to me that he was the angel that had joined me and my trio of angels as we were sitting in my lounge. This is the angel that was taking me on the journey through the veil and into the world of spirit. He said to me that the human form has no idea how large the spirit world is. He said we feel that our earth is a large place but he said that it pales into insignificance compared to the magnitude of the spirit world. He did say, however, that while the spirit world is extreme in size, it is a much simpler and tranquil life in the world of spirit compared to the complexity of life on earth.

I was looking around me and I was rather amazed to see large buildings and homes all about me. It was as though in the distance was a city, and closer to me was a whole host of houses. I asked the angel were we indeed in the spirit world and if so what were the houses and buildings doing there.

He laughed at this and asked where I thought that spirits lived. I said that I understood the human being was of a material form and therefore needed houses and buildings in which to live and go about their daily tasks, but I said I could not comprehend how there would be the equivalent of those houses and buildings in the spirit world itself. He said that there was much to learn, and while he could only show me a brief overview of life in the spirit world, he said that it was important that I just accepted what I was being shown at face value and that I did not try to analyse it or investigate any specific area.

Feeling totally confused, having seen the buildings that I saw, I readily accepted this advice. He pointed out a large building, quite some considerable distance away. The building was beige in colour and must have been about twenty storeys high. He said that we were going to go to that building and it would be the start of the learning process he wished to take me through. He also said it was a very apt place for us to start because it was called the Halls of Learning.

I wondered how we were going to get there because it did seem quite some distance away. He took a couple of steps closer to me and stood right by me on my left-hand side. He asked me to close my eyes for a second and that I duly did. I then felt what was almost like a gust of wind across my face and I immediately opened my eyes to find myself standing in the foyer of a building. The angel was still standing next to me and I asked him how that happened and where we were. He smiled and said to me that one of the first lessons I needed to learn was that movement in the spirit world could take the form of many things. On many occasions, spirits would choose to walk around from point A to point B and to just chat with their friends and colleagues, going about their daily business, but he also said spirits possessed the ability to travel from point A to point B just by thought. He said that while I would be taught to do that when it was my turn to pass over to the other side, on this occasion I would tag along with his energy in his particular travels. I said to the angel that this was almost a spiritual form of somebody giving somebody else a piggyback, and we both laughed at that.

The angel said to me that there were many buildings in the spirit world, which were where spirits congregated for their own development. He said we had started our journey in the Halls of Learning, but there were also many forms of convalescent homes for spirits that had recently arrived after leaving earth at their own death. There were many forms of artistic and cultural centres for spirits to develop and that all spirits, in some form or another, chose to spend some of their time developing their artistic abilities, whether that be in art itself, or in learning to play musical instruments, or in many other forms of artistic pursuits.

The angel said to me that I needed to understand that time does not exist in the world of spirit. Even to this day, I still have trouble with that concept, understanding how time itself is an illusion, but that is exactly what it is. It *is* an illusion. In the spirit world, time does not exist and there is therefore an infinite amount of time for spirits to carry out their work. They have an infinity of time; there are always other spirits available to help in whatever way is needed; you can be alone or you can be with others. The choice is yours. But the most incredible thing to realise is that anything that any spirit ever needs can be fulfilled just by sending out a thought for others to assist you.

I did not ask the angel's name and perhaps that was to my credit because it demonstrated that I was out of my analytical mind, but in another way I wish I had asked his name because I have not seen him again since he gave me what I suppose I can call a tour of the spirit world.

The first thing I noticed in the Halls of Learning was the amount of spirits that there were walking about, doing whatever it was they were all up to. I noticed how polite and pleasant everybody was to each other. Everybody seemed to know everybody else, everybody smiled at everybody else and everybody was there to help in whatever way was possible. This did seem indeed a setting of sheer paradise.

The angel could tell that I was looking at the other spirits in great amazement at the way that they were exchanging pleasantries with each other and the angel said to me that I should not be surprised at this, as it is customary for spirits always to be polite to each other and that generally they had their closer friends, just as you would do in domestic circles on earth.

The angel took me into one of the rooms in the Halls of Learning and showed me some information regarding spiritual progression. I was reading the literature that he showed me in the same way that one would read a book. It gave examples of how some human beings had traumatic deaths and that their spirits, upon arriving in the spirit world, had gone into something similar to convalescent homes or hospitals. You are never alone in these places; there is the equivalent of a nursing team supporting you at all times, you are helped in the transition from the earthly world to the spirit world and you are given a lot of information to enable you to adjust as quickly as possible. When you are ready, and it is only when you are ready, you are then met by others that you will have known of old. This may be members of your family, it may be your ancestors, or it may even be some of your current friends who have passed before you, but you will always be met by those that are truly nearest and dearest to you and they will help you to adjust to life in the spirit world.

It was clear from some of the information that I was reviewing that the spirit world is indeed a journey of evolution. Everybody has the desire to help and assist with others but equally everybody has a desire to develop their own soul and spirit even further. That is why the Halls of Learning are obviously such a busy place.

From the literature that I was looking at, it was also obvious to me that the home that you always sought on earth but could never quite achieve is readily at your disposal, should that be what you require in the spirit world. Whether you chose a humble dwelling or whether you chose a much larger dwelling, the dwelling could be of your choice, with the land and gardens around it being as you require. There is never a shortage of what we could refer to as earthly tradesmen or earthly gardeners and all are readily available to help you in the spirit world to develop the home and the gardens of your dreams.

This is an incredible thought, but a lovely thought too. I know, for example, that Jackie has the vision of having a beautiful little home in the spirit world with an equally beautiful garden attached to it and in that garden can be the spirit of all the animals that she has ever owned and, indeed, all the animals that would want to live with Jackie in those beautiful surroundings.

There is a wonderful piece of writing that you can readily find on the internet called 'Rainbow Bridge' and this gives a very emotional account of what happens to the spirits of animals when they pass over to the other side. In essence, when a human being in spirit form has a longing to be reunited with their departed pets, waiting on the other side of that rainbow bridge is indeed the spirit of your pets. When you pass and you yourself cross that bridge, you are once again reunited with the spirit of your beloved animal. There you can be as one and run and play in the woods if that is what you want to do, or just be in the company of one another once again. Certainly from Jackie's perspective, her beautiful house in the spirit world and her beautiful garden in the spirit world will have a very large amount of animal spirits awaiting her arrival. She will be knocked down in the rush of the hundreds of paws from dogs, cats and other animals that will be bounding across her garden to greet her when she arrives.

The angel then said to me that we needed to move on into one of the other rooms and look at some more information concerning life in the spirit world. I must admit I was truly amazed at the sheer scale of life in the spirit world. Scale, yes, but complexity no. You see, there was no complexity at all in the spirit world; everything was peaceful and tranquil, everybody seemed to be happy going about their ways and everybody seemed to have a purpose. This indeed was heaven.

While moving from one room to the other, I asked the angel how the spirits decided what it was that they wanted to do. He said to me they could do whatever it was that their soul growth demanded. If they chose to follow a path of music and arts, then that was fine. If they chose a path of learning, then there were massive libraries in the spirit world where they could learn everything that they ever wanted to know from the wealth of books and writings that were available.

He also said to me that many of the great scientists of old do exactly the same work in the spirit world; they continue to develop themselves and the products that they are working on and some of these products are passed back to people on earth, either through thought forms or in other ways, which come across to the human being as bright ideas. I could clearly see now how the words 'divine intervention' or 'a gift from heaven' or 'a divine spark' could apply. I have no doubt whatsoever that many of our innovative thoughts on the planet earth have been given to us by a thought form from those in the spirit world.

I was then taken into a room where the angel said to me that I would be shown some information regarding the ability of thought in the spirit world, as opposed to the ability of thought in an earthly confinement. I cannot recall the exact words that were written but I suppose the biggest difference was the fact that, while earth had material and solid conditions imposed upon it and therefore that influenced our thoughts, in the spirit world there was no such thing as a material item to inhibit our thought process. Whatever is created on earth has, of course, to be thought about, then it has to be planned and then diary dates made surrounding it, perhaps drawings undertaken or architecture devised, and then perhaps machinery and tools are made available in order to construct whatever it is that is needed. Generally, this is quite an elaborate process. Whereas, in the spirit world, as soon as a thought is made about a particular requirement, the product is duly delivered.

I said to the angel that this was indeed an incredible difference and I asked him how spirits constructed their thoughts prior to the object being obtained. I said to him that this would be an incredible ability to have, everything you thought you wanted being suddenly provided. He smiled at that and said it was not a free-for-all as such, but that for anything a spirit desired, if the spirit then thought along those lines, then the object would duly arrive.

He said an important point at this time: he said that spirits are not interested in personal gain. There is no money, there is no finance, there is no ego and therefore the only thing that spirit would ever desire is something that would benefit themselves and other spirits.

He gave an example of somebody wanting a particularly beautiful garden. He said that garden would be provided and the spirit gardeners as such would tend to the garden for them, and he said that while the individual spirit would benefit from being in the presence of such beautiful gardens, so would other spirits that passed the area and could look admiringly at that particular garden. He said it was therefore a gain for all concerned. I began to then have a better understanding of evolution within the spirit world, unaffected by the materiality, ego and greed that are present on earth. This place is indeed nirvana.

The angel then said to me that we were going to visit a place of worship, but he told me that there were no religious boundaries in this worship. Everybody, no matter what earthly faith, creed, colour, denomination, sex or sexual inclination, had exactly the same purpose in the place of worship. They went to the place of worship, which I suppose we can call a church, just to give their gratitude and thanks for everything that is provided in the spirit world.

The angel told me that whereas I had previously been shown and taught about the nine levels of the angel hierarchy, the same type of thing applied in the spirit world. There are many levels in the spirit world and your soul and your soul group will dictate the level to which you are best suited. The angel said to me that there is a golden rule, which in essence is a spiritual law. No spirit can go to any level that is higher than their own level, but any spirit at a higher level can go down to any other level to assist or to help out wherever that is required. The angel said to me that, on many occasions, a higher-level spirit or a celestial being would come down from one of the higher levels and give a talk or a lecture at the place of worship and share even more love among those that were present. These particular visits were always seen and greeted with great excitement among the attendees.

The angel continued by telling me that religion on earth has gone totally haywire. It is the cause of much greed and corruption, it is the cause of many wars and it is the cause of much division on earth. There is no such divide in the spirit world, and there are some people on earth in very high places in different religions that know the truth but choose to conceal that truth in order to control the masses. This is indeed a despicable thing to do. The control that many religions hold over people and the fear that that creates is indeed totally unjust and is not required. True spirituality that I have seen beyond the veil, where 'all for one and one for all' is an underpinning fact, sadly appears to be beyond us while we are in human form. What a better place the earth would be if only we could return to our roots and all acknowledge that we are all part of the oneness that is the creator.

I said to the angel that while I could see some vast differences in the way that spirits go about life within the spirit world, there was also some similarity inasmuch as there were houses and buildings much the same as there was on earth. I understood that these could be constructed by thought and that there were the equivalent of tradesman voluntarily going about their activities, supporting what I suppose I could refer to as the spiritual infrastructure, and I asked the angel what other major differences there were between the spirit world and life on earth.

He smiled and said that food was a classic example of the difference. In the spirit world, there is no need for food. Spirits are sustained by the light; their own life force comes from the light and therefore food is not required. They did occasionally sample the fruits of nature, such as apples and peaches, but these were only ever sampled so as just to have the appearance of the taste of the fruit. Spirits have no organs as such, and therefore no digestive system, so food is not required. The angel contrasted this with life on earth, where there is a whole industry involved in food processing, not least the growing of the food, the manufacturing of the food, the retail outlets, and so on.

He also mentioned clothing as another example. There is no need whatsoever to design or to manufacture clothes. Clothes are also provided by thought. I also then threw in myself the difference between the transport arrangements in the spirit world compared to earth, with transport consisting of either walking whatever distance you chose to walk, or through thought; there was no such thing as a transport infrastructure. I began to think more laterally while I was talking to the angel. There would be no shops as there is no financial system. Spirits never need to purchase anything. With that, the angel looked at me and said that I was beginning to grasp some of the fundamental differences between the spirit world and the earth world.

I said to the angel that I couldn't help noticing how everybody was dressed in clothing that was flowing and it almost consisted of gowns of silk-like material. The angel said to me that spirit clothing was totally different to earthly clothing. Their clothing is outer attire but it enables the spirit to be totally free in all of their activities and earthly clothing is totally different to spiritual clothing. Certainly I could tell that from looking at the colours, inasmuch as there were all manner of bright colours.

We then moved into a different room in the Halls of Learning and it would be hard to summarise some of the content of this room. The angel said to me that the room consisted of all the thousands of years of history of the planet earth, from the most minute detail showing scientific advancement and scientific breakthroughs, to medical treatments and surgical procedures, to manufacturing processes and discoveries. Any question that you ever had concerning what man has achieved on earth could be answered in this one room in this Hall of Learning.

The angel told me and showed me how to raise questions and have them answered. It was as though there was a small screen in front of me, although there was nothing physical in front of me at all. All I had to do was think my question and there before me, on something almost like a television screen in appearance, would come the answers. That answer could consist of some text, it could consist of an image being displayed in front of me, or it could even consist of a spirit standing before me, answering the question, or showing me the answer to the question. This is certainly beyond human comprehension, but my word, this was a very powerful and interesting sight.

When we left the room, I asked the angel how spirits decide what it is that they want to do. He laughed at that and said spirits decide themselves what they want to do. They decide what they choose to do. The angel said to me that, on earth, the vast majority of the population work hard, and do whatever it is they have to do in order to sustain their physical and material life, whereas in the spirit world, you truly can do what is your heart's desire. If your desire is to live and work with animals, such as Jackie's is, then that can be readily achieved. If your desire is to be a musician or an author or an artist, then again, that can readily be achieved. Those that have a passion and a love for outdoor exercises such as gardening, landscaping or hiking, again, all of those can be readily achieved. In essence, whatever is in your heart, whatever is in your soul, whatever it is that would bring you passion in life, whatever it is that would bring you love in your life, then that is what awaits you in the spirit world. There is no such thing as suffering, there is no such thing as pain, and there is no such thing as grieving. Everything in the spirit world has the baseline of love and the baseline of light. Service to others is what drives all spirits on. The ability to help others, and indeed to help yourself, is a joy that is immeasurable in the spirit world.

This may seem a strange thing to say but it makes me think of when somebody dies on earth, on many headstones you see the words 'rest in peace'. How ironic that statement is. Perhaps that is a good symbol for what happens to the earthly body: if you have had a traumatic and painful life, if you have had many years of suffering and been ravaged by disease, then yes indeed, it is perhaps gratifying to know that your physical body at the time of death truly rests in peace.

But from a spiritual perspective, the total opposite is true: peace prevails totally within the spirit world, for that is all that exists – love and peace – and everything you do is encompassed within those words. But to actually rest in peace would be totally alien to spirits. They love what they do, they love their learning, they love their evolution, they love their drive for service, they love being part of the creator. For that is what awaits us all; whatever pain and suffering we have on earth, whatever hardships we face, whatever difficulties and challenges we have had and we still will have, just know, and know this within every fibre of your being, that what awaits you on the other side of the veil is a life of sheer joy, a life of love and a life of bliss.

With that as a backdrop, we should not all act like lemmings and jump off the nearest cliff, trying to reach that life earlier than we are destined to. We all chose to come to this earth for some reason or another. When you return to the spirit world and you have your own individual review with the angels of powers, then your soul contract and your mission on earth will become clearer, but whatever it is that you asked to do – and remember every-thing that you are facing on earth is brought to you by the challenges that you wish to face – then we should all do whatever it is that we can do in order to make our life and the lives of others on earth as fulfilling as possible. We should all try to find tranquillity on earth and peace in all that we do and not let the stresses and strains of life's challenges get us down. Every challenge should be viewed as a hurdle to overcome; every challenge can help in our soul growth. For those of us that have nothing, embrace it; try to live from the heart rather than the head, try to accept whatever you have, try to make the best of what you have. Equally, for those that have everything that they could ever desire, enjoy it; embrace it also. For those that have lots, perhaps they could consider donating some of their wealth to charities to do good on earth, because anything that you do that is from the heart in support of others will be repaid to you tenfold, in terms of your own spiritual growth.

Obviously everything has to be done for the right reasons. If you are truly giving to others for the pleasure that that can bring to them and the joy that that can bring to them, then that is the right intention. If you are doing it purely for self-satisfaction, then that is the wrong intention. A kind, generous deed, whether that be financial or otherwise, is fulfilling for all concerned, both for the giver and the receiver. Certainly in today's age, there is a wide disparity between the extreme wealth of the drug companies and the major corporations compared to the starving peoples of Africa, for example. Mankind will never find true peace and inner peace all of the time those disparities exist. It is beholden on all of us to play our part in trying to bring more light into the world, whether that is by smiling at somebody you see in the street, whether that is by giving a pound to a *Big Issue* seller, whether it is just holding a door open for somebody, or whether it is just saying please and thank you in a shop – whatever it is, every small step goes some way to making this world a better place.

The angel then took me out of the Halls of Learning and we went into one of the vast libraries where there were books on many subjects. It would be impossible to describe the size of the libraries and the amount of books available. I did notice that many of the books were historical books written by great authors, but also many of the books were books written by those in spirit. I asked the angel why some of the books that were written by those in spirit, those that had great knowledge of both the earth world and the spirit world, were not more readily passed down to those on earth, to help us in our way of living. For example, there must be many medical breakthroughs that have been written about in the spirit world that would indeed help us enormously on earth. I am certainly not going to go into any political lecture here but it was clear to me that some of the major drug corporations and some of the behind-the-scenes political associations probably would have no interest in bringing those developments to the earth at this particular time. We are still a race that is hugely and highly motivated by financial greed. One day, I truly hope that will change and that change will be the first step of the re-emergence of man. Mankind can then develop into the race that we should have been already: a race full of love and compassion for others. Perhaps we are light years away from that, but that day will come.

The angel then said to me that we needed to go outside and experience some of the other spiritual sights that would be shown to me. We had a wonderful walk through some woods and some gardens and we were always greeted by smiling faces throughout our journey. I was shown into a convalescent home to see some recently arrived spirits and I really appreciated being shown that, as I truly saw the other side of my spirit rescue work. I could almost envisage the spirit rescue work that I carry out on earth as being the 'departure lounge' for spirits, and the convalescent homes and some of the other places that spirits first go to after death as the 'arrivals lounge'.

Thinking about that analogy, it seems very appropriate. I was also taken to what I could best describe as a musical festival hall, where there were many large auditoriums with people playing all sorts of musical instruments, as well as a whole array of people listening to the music being played. I could tell this was giving great pleasure to many.

The angel said to me that there were many other places that he could take me, for example the art exhibitions and suchlike, as well as many other cultural learning centres, but that the time had come to return home. I must admit I felt so at home that I had almost forgotten that I was just being shown around as what I could best describe as a guest. It seemed almost alien to me to leave such a loving environment. The angel said to me that I would be shown more at an appropriate date but that I had already been shown enough to enable me to fulfil my spirit rescue work with a great deal more conviction than had hitherto been the case. I accepted that comment without reservation.

The angel asked me to follow him across a particular field and to walk alongside him. We must have walked for a matter of minutes in earth time and we were having quite an in-depth conversation about the things that I had learnt and the things that I had been shown. Suddenly I was once again aware of travelling, as though I had taken one step out of the field and into a tunnel of light. The kaleidoscope of colours was again all around me and I suddenly felt myself becoming rather disorientated, and before anything else happened, I was suddenly aware that I was sitting in the armchair in my lounge.

The angel was speaking to me in his soft, melancholy tones and he asked me to keep my eyes closed and just to become aware of my human body and to breathe deeply and in a relaxed manner. I did feel extremely lightheaded and rather nauseated, but the most prevalent feeling was one of extreme weight. I felt incredibly heavy. I did not realise just how light the whole feeling was when I was in the spirit world and it was incredibly different to then be back on the earth plane, with its extreme density and dull vibration.

The angel said to me that he would be returning to where he had come from and he said it was a pleasure to show me what he had shown me. I still had my eyes closed but I thanked him from the bottom of my heart for all that he had shown me and all he had taught me and I said to him that I hoped that we would meet again in the near future. He did not answer that. He just vanished and I was suddenly aware that I was back with my trio of angels.

Chrystal asked me to open my eyes and we spoke for a few minutes while I adjusted to being back in my earthly body. With that, Chrystal and Amhiel said that they also were leaving and would return in a matter of days once I had assimilated the information that I had been given. I had quite a long chat with Bella, who was her normal, supportive self, and she was much more concerned about me, rather than hearing about what I had experienced. I remember getting more and more excited as I wanted to tell her everything that I had been shown, but Bella just asked me to be still, to be calm and to chat about other things. She said there would be many weeks, months and years ahead for me to be able to consolidate all that I had been shown and to build upon that consolidated level with new information that would be provided to me at the appropriate times.

I was genuinely pleased to hear that my learning and development would continue. To know that development was being carried out by angels is indeed a very humbling thought.

What Next?

It did indeed take me a few days to comprehend all that I had been shown during the visit beyond the veil, and indeed even to this day, a few months later, I still have further recollections of some of the information I was given. I am truly grateful that I was given the opportunity of the visit and I know from further discussions with Chrystal that I will be going beyond the veil on future occasions to be shown even more information that will help me on my spiritual journey as well as hopefully helping many others, either by the spirit rescue work that I undertake or by other spiritual teachings that I will be giving at some time in the future.

So here we are at this particular chapter, which is 'what next?' Well, for me, I would like to think that the angels know that I am learning some of the lessons that they are giving me. For example, the old me would have spelled out in this chapter everything that I now intend to undertake on my spiritual path and to use my analytical mind to plan that. Well, Chrystal, Bella and Amhiel, this is for you. I do not intend to think of what my next steps are going to be. I am truly in your hands: whatever the angels and spirit would like me to do on this earth, it would be my pleasure to do so. I await your instructions!

Certainly, in the meantime, I will be continuing with the spirit rescue work that I am undertaking. I find great pleasure in doing that and I know from a discussion I have recently had with Chrystal that I will be undertaking literally hundreds of spirit rescues during the next year or so. This will be a pleasure to undertake on behalf of the angels.

So from a spiritual perspective, I will try to continue to lead my life in a light worker's way. I will undertake the spirit rescue work whenever the opportunity presents itself. I will chat to my trio of angels at every opportunity, and most importantly of all, I will keep myself fully open to the many methods of communication that the angels and spirits use to communicate with me. Doing that will ensure that I pick up their messages and follow the next steps that they would like me to take. I already know that my spirit rescue work will continue until my dying day on earth and may well even continue when I am in spirit. In essence, I will transfer from seeing people off at the departure lounge at this end to being employed at the arrivals lounge at the other end! Either way, it is truly fulfilling work.

From an earthly perspective, it has been a pleasure to write this book on behalf of the angels and if one person can receive any benefit from having read it, then all of the many hours involved will have been worth it. I know that the angels wanted me to write this book and for that reason I know that there is at least one person out there who needs to read the book for their own spiritual progression. Now, whether that is one person, whether that is one hundred and one people, whether it is a thousand and one people, or whether it is a million people, I hope whoever reads this book can receive encouragement and support from it. The angels are there to help you, and they can help you in every facet of your life. All you have to do is ask and be ready to accept the angels with open arms into your life. They can transform your life; they can help you on your own spiritual progression and on your own spiritual path – just allow them in and allow them to help you.

I have recently started to attend an art class, and as I have mentioned previously, I have zero ability in terms of drawing or painting, but it does provide me some pleasure and relief from the stresses that we all currently face and I hope one day that I will be able to paint my trio of angels so that I have a physical record of the beauty that they are, and I also readily recall the spirit lady who visited me and asked me to paint her. It would be my pleasure to do this as soon as my competence has grown!

So in closing, for those spirits out there that need any form of assistance or spirit rescue, I truly hope to be in a position to be able to help you in whatever way I can. For the angels out there, thank you so much for blessing my life, thank you so much for always being there for me and thank you so much for always being there for mankind.

For the many spirit guides out there that are trying to help us in the human race, please continue to do so. We need every ounce of your assistance.

And finally, for those of you out there that have read this book, my heartfelt thanks for taking the time to read it, and if any of it can be used as a way of illuminating your own spiritual path, then I am greatly thankful for the opportunity to have been able to help in that way. Remember, in all of us, in every living being, there is an element of the god presence; we all have an element of the creator within us, we all have a portion of the original light within us. Now let us use that light for the benefit of mankind, for the benefit of the human race, for the benefit of the planet earth and for the benefit of the universe.

May the angels always walk by your side.

1316185R0

Printed in Great Britain by
Amazon.co.uk, Ltd.,
Marston Gate.